# The Last One Hundred and Eighty Days

*A Chronicle of a Non-profit*
*Independent Charter School's Struggle to Survive in*
*One of the Largest School Districts in the Country*

D1744589

## Keitha D. Burnett, Ph.D.

outskirts
press

*Painting by Carlos Navarro*

The late Mr. Allen Lawrence (August 4, 1915-December 29, 2010) and the late Mrs. Roxie Lawrence (October 4, 1919-February 9, 2004)

*Dedicated to the memory of my parents who are the inspiration for Lawrence Academy, and the students along with my husband, Michael and my children, Melanie and Michael II.*

# ABBREVIATIONS:

| | |
|---|---|
| CELLA | Comprehensive English Language Learners Assessment |
| COFFO | Coalition of Florida's Farm Workers |
| CSO | Charter School Operations |
| DAC | District Advisory Committee (Title I) |
| DI/HOT | Differentiated Instruction/Higher Order Thinking |
| E.O.C. | End-of-Course |
| ELL | English Language Learners |
| FCAT | Florida Comprehensive Assessment Test |
| FCIM | Florida Continuous Improvement Model |
| FTE | Full-time Equivalent |
| IFC | Instructional Focus Calendar |
| PD | Professional Development |
| PMP | Progress Monitoring Plan |
| RTI | Response to Intervention |
| SPED | Special Education |

# TABLE OF CONTENTS

Preface .................................................................................i

Introduction ..........................................................................v

Background .........................................................................vii

August 5, 2005     (A Small Miracle) ....................xii

Quest for Academic
Excellence     (An Overview) .................... xxiii

July 16, 2011     (A Day of Reckoning
at the District Office) ........... xxv

Part 1: Strength and Wisdom ...............................................1

2011: August 1-7     (Time for Reflection) ...............3

2011: August 8-14     (Teacher Preparation
Surpasses Lease Issues) ..............7

2011: August 15-21     (Classroom Preparation) .........10

2011: August 22-31     (Beginning of School!!!) ..........11

2011: September 1-11     (The Leadership Team) ..........13

2011: September 12-18     (The State Visit and a
Jewel on the Sideline) ..............16

2011: September 19-25     (From Open House to
Board Meeting and
Everything In Between) ..........19

2011: September 26-30     (Following the Valdes
Shuffle) ................................22

2011: October 1-7        (From Saturday School
to Budgeting Meeting) ...........28

2011: October 8-14       (Making It Work)....................30

2011: October 15-21     (Balancing Family, Lawrence
Academy Elementary,
Lawrence Middle, and
Lawrence Academy Senior).....32

2011: October 22-28     (Red Ribbon Week Infused
with Writing and Data
Chats) ....................................36

2011: October 29-31     (Intervention Program and
Phase 1 of Saturday
Academy) ...............................37

2011: November 1-6     (More Planning, More
Meetings) ...............................38

2011: November 7-13    (Founders' Week) ...................40

2011: November 14-20   (More Testing...More
Meetings) ...............................49

2011: November 21-27   (The Eagle's Nest, A Labor
of Love in the Midst of
Directives)...............................50

2011: November 28-30   (Efforts to Build a
Community Coalition) ..........53

2011: December 1-4      (Seeking Peace in the
Eye of the Storm) ...................54

2011: December 5-11     (From Idealism to Realism) ......55

2011: December 12-18    (In spite of....Celebrating
    the Holiday Season) ...............65

2011: December 19-25    (One More Tutorial Session
    Just Before the Holidays)........68

2011: December 26-31    (A Cure for the Blues) ...........70


Part II: Countdown to FCAT ...............................75

2012: January 2-8    (Ready, Set, Go...Phase II
    Tutorials)...............................77

2012: January 9-15    (Too Many Battles)................81

2012: January 16-22    (Dr. Martin Luther King's
    Birthday)...............................85

2012: January 23-29    (A Little Time for our
    Seniors) ...............................88

2012: January 30-31    (More assessments and
    Preparation for the Renewal) ....89

2012: February 1-5    (The Renewal Meeting)..........90

2012: February 6-12    (Intervention, Reinforcement,
    and more Reinforcement).....100

2012: February 13-19    (Proficiency trumps
    Valentine's Day and Black
    History Month)...................100

2012: February 20-29    (Days Before the FCAT
    Writing Assessment) .............101

2012: March 1-4    (The Parent Task Force)........102

2012: March 5-11       (Preparation for CELLA
Testing, Title 1 Audit,
Mock FCAT 2.0 Testing,
and Senior Activities) ..........103

2012: March 12-18     (Turbo Tutorials) ..................105

2012: March 19-25     (School Lockdown) ..............105

2012: March 26-30     (Trip to Bogota, Columbia)..107

2012: April 2-8         (Countdown Begins!!) ..........110

April 9-15             (In the Midst of Testing
and Monitoring...A PREP
Rally) ...................................111

2012: April 16-22      (Could it be a Set-up?) .........113

2012: April 23-30      (Winding Down) .................122

2012: May 1- 6         (Family Time) ......................123

2012: May 7-13        (Not a State Visit, but a
Fieldtrip to the Library)........124

2012: May 14-20       (Activities for the Soul).........124

2012: May 21-27       (It's All About Family) ..........126

2012: May 28-31       (Kindergarten Graduation).....128

2012: June 1-10        (End of School Activities,
A Surprise Teacher's
Confession, and Ending
with a World-Class
Graduation 2012) .................129

June 11-August 1     (The Verdict).......................141


Reflections and Final Note ...............................145

Appendices........................................................161
    Appendix A.............................................163
    Appendix B.............................................164
    Appendix C.............................................166
    Appendix D.............................................168

# PREFACE

This book chronicles the challenges of operating a nonprofit independent charter school, serving a population with ninety-nine percent of the students on free or reduced lunch in one of the largest school districts in America. It details the operation of Lawrence Academy Elementary (founded 2008) from July 2011 to August 2012 during the most critical year in the history of the school. Its intent is not an indictment against any specific person or organization; instead, its intent is to highlight some systemic problems that indirectly affect educators in the trenches.

Founded at a time when the state of Florida was transitioning yearly to new testing standards, Lawrence Academy Elementary (founded 2008) had fallen short of a passing grade for two consecutive years and was on the brink of closure. Lawrence Academy Middle (founded 2005) and Lawrence Academy Senior High (founded 2007) shared a new state-of-the art facility with the elementary, but the fate of the elementary threatened the two other schools. The schools shared a facility, and siblings attending the upper schools often took responsibility for overseeing their younger siblings before and after school.

It is the premise of this book that it is nearly impossible to make a significant difference statistically in the performance of low socio-economic and academic performance **within** a short timeframe on standardized tests without resorting to data manipulation or other undesirable means. It further suggests that in the quest for accountability, the richness inherent in the education process, particularly at schools that have a high percentage of low-performing students has been lost. We are failing to "educate" all our children. It also suggests that the "creaming effect" that is occurring in poor neighborhoods—that is the skimming of the best students to attend magnet or other county schools—contributes to the erosion of our education system, leaving the perception as a whole that some schools are doing better than others. Following rules and guidelines is not enough to truly address the needs of the neediest students and this often leaves educators drained and disillusioned when desired results cannot be attained.

In my self-evaluation, I have studied a spectrum of educational philosophies and experienced a range of emotions while taking into account my strengths and weaknesses. My journey in education has brought me to an understanding that failure is not always quantifiable. My experiences over the past ten years have enabled me to view education from a "third eye," reaching beyond the limitations of economic, political, and social constraints. I believe we are indirectly plagued by our "one best method" way of thinking and our method, which stifles and limits creativity. Long-term goals related to promoting creativity and ingenuity are compromised to short-term goals related to increasing standardized test scores. What is needed is a serious call to action that includes a plan to reclaim a sense of pride in our community and our neighborhood schools that focuses on individualized learning. The final note of this book offers several pathways to a solution. It is my hope the insight I have gained will redirect local, state, and national leaders to move in a direction that will lead to a more comprehensive approach to educational policy.

Beyond my immediate family to whom I have dedicated this book, I would like to acknowledge Ms. King, the Governing Board Chair; Ms. Lula Pearson, the Vice-Chair, and wife of the late Mr. Eddie Pearson (first Governing Board Chair); former and present board members; the Lawrence Academy administrators, Ms. Valdes and Mr. Katz; the late Dr. Cassandra Middlebrooks, former lead teacher and Humanities Department Chair; and teachers, staff, students, and parents who have all shared a part of their lives to bring a mere dream into existence. In my life, I know I will always be indebted to the significant educators in my life; the late Mrs. Martha Townsend, the late Ms. Julia Foster, Mrs. Dean Whicker, Dr. James Svara, Drs. Robert and Mary Kweit, the late Dr. Stephen Loveless, Dr. Fred Newman, Dr. Ann Witte, and Dr. Milan Dluhy. I cannot underestimate the significance of my "virtual" morning tea discussions with my beloved niece, Tachelle Wilkes who helped me in development of this book.

# INTRODUCTION

Subsequent to the background, this book is divided into three parts. Part 1, *Strength and Wisdom*, covers the time period from the opening of school in 2011 until winter break. Part II, *Countdown to FCAT*, covers the time period after winter break until the close of school in June 2012. Most readers and particularly educators can understand and appreciate the significance of the organization of this book, particularly with the increase in the importance of accountability on standardized testing.

The book encompasses the culture of Lawrence Academy through the author's weekly diary that is supplemented and supported by documents such as contractual agreements, agendas, minutes, memos, speeches, and informal interviews of administrators, teachers, staff and students. Part III gives a comprehensive and thoughtful reflection and final note that includes the progression of Lawrence Academy until the fall of 2014. Additionally, three political cartoons were created specifically for this book to capture and highlight critical educational issues as well as important lessons that were learned.

This book mirrors as closely as possible not only the events, but also the emotions, thoughts, and relationships that were relevant during this time period. Some names were changed or omitted for the purpose of not detracting from the relevant issues that are raised in the book.

# BACKGROUND

July 16, 2011 was the day of reckoning for Lawrence Academy Elementary School. An informal hearing was scheduled in room 559 of the school board building to determine whether Lawrence Academy Elementary would remain open. Ms. Althea King, the governing board chair, Ms. Ileana Valdes, the elementary principal, and other supporters including myself awaited the opening of the meeting.

The journey to establish a quality educational institution had been anything but smooth sailing. I tried to concentrate on the initial vision of Lawrence Academy that seemed to elude me at times through the trials and tribulations we had endured. It was comforting at that time to reflect back on those moments of miracle that put Lawrence Academy in motion.

In the fall of 1991, Jacqueline Hinchey-Sipes, principal of Design and Architecture Senior High School, hired me as a social studies teacher. I was impressed that Ms. Hinchey-Sipes was not only the principal, but had written the proposal for the school. I was sold on writing a proposal for my own school from that day forth.

I had always been interested in academic achievement. Instinctively, I felt that academic achievement was determined more intrinsically than extrinsically. In my studies, I was introduced to Albert Bandura's theory of self-efficacy (the degree one feels he/she has influence), which Bandura found played a significant role in academic achievement. As a result, I used Bandura's model to design an economic evaluation of alternative high school settings by assessing the cost-effectiveness of magnet schools v. traditional schools. I found that the impact of a school's academic program does not play as great a role in academic achievement as many may believe, particularly among minorities. However, the variable self-efficacy was significant. Based on these findings, I believed that if self-efficacy could be promoted and cultivated through the curriculum, it would increase academic achievement. I found that much of this self-efficacy could be accomplished through character education.

In the early stages of writing two proposals for Lawrence Academy, it was only my husband, Michael and I working on the groundwork to make Lawrence Academy a reality. In 2002, I visited Frederick Douglas Academy, founded by Dr. Lorraine Monroe in Harlem, New York, to help me with the conceptualization of academic success in the midst of challenges. With great support from my husband, Michael, we put together a proposal for a charter school in September 2004. Lawrence

Academy was incorporated on November 10, 2004. The first formal meeting took place on June 30, 2004 at Florida International University, Ryder Center, and Room 358. Eddie Pearson, former Deputy Superintendent (MDCPS); Dr. Ralph Lewis, former professor of Public Administration (FIU) and Executive Assistant for Strategic Initiatives (MDCPS); Lynda Raheem, Assistant Dean of Undergraduate Advising/FIU College of Business; Sofia Santiesteban, Director of Upward Bound and Pre-College Programs (FIU); Kathy Leahy, Department of Human Relations (Miami-Dade County), and Dr. Richard Campbell (Professor of Science Education) agreed to serve on the governing board. By the second meeting, Mr. Pearson had a prospective building that could be leased. The owner of the building was one of Mr. Pearson's former students, Mr. Jerome Eppinger. Mr. Eddie Pearson was elected to serve as the chairman, and Dr. Ralph Lewis was elected to serve as the vice-chairman. A ten-year contract was secured April 13, 2005.

Lawrence Academy, Inc. was designed to draw on America's full and rich heritage by promoting a strong work ethic and establishing commitment to moral development. The envisioned mission of Lawrence Academy "was to build character in tomorrow's leaders for high school students by cultivating a rigorous and challenging academic environment with a college preparatory curriculum infused with character building techniques, supported through the efforts of the school, family and community." The school was founded on core values, giving students the foundation to tackle vigorous and challenging curriculum, and, further, giving students the tools to be productive citizens. The primary core values were derived from Miami-Dade County's Character Education curriculum, which includes citizenship, cooperation, fairness, honesty, integrity, kindness, pursuit of excellence, respect, and responsibility.

Lawrence Academy was named to honor Mr. Allen Lawrence and the late Mrs. Roxie Lawrence, ordinary people who did extraordinary actions by setting examples for moral behavior and promoting a strong work ethic. They were the parents of eight children who are productive citizens in a wide range of fields such as education, computer technology, business, government, and assembly-line production.

The ultimate goal of Lawrence Academy was for students to value and practice good character and integrity, enabling them to be better decision-makers. Lawrence Academy served grades 6-8, representing Miami-Dade County's diverse population. The Academy was planned for average to slightly below average students who have aspirations of attending a postsecondary institution. The public education system provides additional resources and programs for students that are on either end of the exceptional student spectrum; however, the majority of students fall in the average range. Since there was a need for programs designed for this population, Lawrence Academy expanded to serve the K-5 and 9-12 grade population.

The philosophical basis of the Academy was that learning reaches its optimal level only when students know and expect that all guidelines and policies are set forth as a basis for all decision-making. This requires clear goals and objectives, consistency, monitoring and feedback, clear disciplinary policies, and strong community and parental support. It is essential for the philosophy of the school to shape the culture of school. Interestingly, in the research for my dissertation, I found that the type of school (magnet school, magnet program, or traditional school), was not as significant as the degree of self-efficacy of the students. The degree of self-efficacy is determined by a student's perception of control of his/her environment and circumstances. The study found students at traditional schools with a high degree of self-efficacy generally performed as well academically as their counterparts in magnet programs or magnet schools. Hence, this study suggests that developing a student's self-efficacy is a worthwhile investment academically.

Studies have shown that students with stronger core values possess a greater sense of self-efficacy—in fact, that self-efficacy was one of the major determinants in predicting academic achievement. Therefore, the more character education which permeates the curriculum, the greater the likelihood students will develop a greater sense of self-efficacy, one of the major determinants of academic achievement. Students need support from all vested stakeholders. It can be inferred that students, teachers and administrators can be more productive in an environment that promotes mutual respect and support.

***The importance of character education extends beyond academic achievement.*** In the Florida City/Homestead area, the majority of households consist of either single parents employed full-time, or two parents employed full-time. In either case, this equates to less time for children to spend with their parent(s), who traditionally have been the primary shapers of character. Many times, children are unsupervised after school, spending time watching television, playing video or computer games, or just "hanging out" with friends. We have seen too often, the deadly consequences to unsupervised play. Tragically, it is not until then that we think about the importance of character education in our schools.

The social, ethical, and emotional development of young people is just as important as their academic development. As Theodore Roosevelt stated, "To educate a man in mind and not in morals is to educate a menace to society." Good workers, citizens, parents and neighbors all have their roots in good character. Therefore, it is critical to create schools that simultaneously promote academic and character development. The next challenge and one of the most difficult was the securing of a safe facility.

## August 5, 2005 (A Small Miracle)

I was rushing to the county inspection building to determine the status of 777 West Palm Drive. Jerome, the owner of the building, had promised that everything was in place, but I knew there was too much work that needed to be done on the building to have classes ready for Monday, August 8th. I knew I would have to contact the parents if the inspection building was not ready. Mr. Pearson, the governing board chair, had coached me to play everything to the end, but this was definitely pushing my buttons.

After passing by the building twice, I finally arrived. The parking lot was so crowded that I had to park a good distance from it.

Once inside, it was wall to wall people. I realized I not only knew very little about the process, I didn't even know where to go. I finally reached the right office, only to encounter a long line. It was close to 12:00 noon. How in the world could I have everything ready for the opening of school on Monday, August 8th?

After more than thirty minutes, I reached the front of the line and inquired as to the status of the site plans for 777 West Palm Drive in Florida City, Florida. The clerk asked for the site plan number, which I had never been given.

Sensing my urgency and sheer desperation, the clerk softened to some extent, "What was that address again?"

"777 West Palm Drive, Florida City, Florida," I said.

"Who would have submitted the plans?"

"Jerome Eppinger," I quickly replied.

The gentleman left to research the status of the building, and my heart began to sink when it took over ten minutes. I knew this could not mean good news. I braced myself for the worst, while simultaneously praying for a miracle.

"Ma'am, there are no approved plans," he told me. "There are some plans pending approval, but that is it."

"Are you sure? Is there anything I can do to find out more about this?" I asked.

"Well, you can call Chief Donde. He can give you more information. His number is (305) 222-2332."

I already knew the name. The previous week, he had told Jerome, when I was at the building, that he needed to follow the appropriate process and submit the plans to get approval instead of doing the renovations and expecting the renovations to be approved. Mr. Pearson had inquired about the renovations, but Jerome had assured him that he had everything under control. But, as time began to dwindle to hours, it became evident that Jerome was a fast talker.

Hurrying out the door, I tried to find the most private place to make a phone call to Chief Donde. I saw a bench under a tree on the side of the building that I thought would give some privacy. I began dialing the number as I approached the tree. By the time I was sitting down, Chief Donde answered the phone; I was at a loss for words.

"Chief Donde, this is Keitha Burnett. I will be the new tenant for the building at 777 West Palm Drive. Can you tell me what is going on with the building? Has it been approved?"

"I told the owner over and over again that he has to follow the guidelines for submitting renovations, and he refuses to listen," he said. "There has been a lot of work done on the building, but there is no way that building can be ready Monday morning for the opening of school."

The only thing that I heard was there was no way that the building could be ready for Monday. I could only think about the countless hours I spent night after night writing the application for the school and the effort I expended choosing the best and brightest for our governing board. Just like that… it was gone.

I had forgotten that Chief Donde was on the phone. "Oh, I'm sorry, I'm just very upset right now," I told him. I disconnected the phone and walked quickly to my van. As I sat in my van, I began to talk to God. "Now God," I said, "I know you said you would not leave me, nor forsake me, and you would provide for all of my needs. Unless I am missing something here, I need a building. Lord, God, I know you would not put me out here like this…. I need your guidance."

I called my husband, Michael, and he encouraged me to go to the building and just see if perhaps there was some miscommunication. While I was talking to Michael, there was someone that kept calling, but I decided to continue talking to Michael.

Around the time I arrived at the building, Dr. Helen McGuire, from the District Charter School Office (CSO) drove up. She parked, stepped out of her car, and walked up to me. "So how are things going?

"We weren't able at get a permit and school is on Monday," I said.

Dr. McGuire looked around and said, "With all these offices around here, there must be one that has a current fire permit so you can open on Monday.

I saw Jerome walking out of one of the offices, and we approached him and asked if there were any vacant office spaces with a current fire permit. To my surprise, Jerome informed us that the Job Training Center just moved out, and the space was vacant. He opened the building, which had a reception area, four classrooms, several offices and a small kitchen. Jerome unpinned the fire permit and the certificate of occupancy from the wall and handed it to Dr. McGuire.

Looking at me, she said, "Wow, today is your blessed day. It doesn't expire until October. Dr. Burnett, I think this will be perfect for your opening day of school. Do you have access to a computer and a fax? We need to let the charter school office know that you will be able to open on Monday."

"Wow, this is great! Let's go for it," I said.

Jerome led us to the Department of Children and Families and introduced us to Carlos who allowed us to use his computer and the office fax. In the process, Mr. Pearson, former deputy superintendent of Miami-Dade County Public Schools, and now Governing Board Chair of Lawrence Academy, walked into the office just about the time we needed him to sign a letter stating our change of location.

"Mr. Pearson, how did you know we were here?" I asked.

Smiling, he said, "Willie told me that I might find you in here." Willie was Jerome's handyman. He opened the building, kept the parking lot clean and did the general maintenance around the property.

"Hi, Mr. Pearson. My name is Helen McGuire. I am from the Charter School Office. Wow, all of us are in the right place at the right time. I need you to sign this letter stating that

Lawrence Academy will be opening at 751 West Palm Drive instead of 777 West Palm Drive," she said.

As Mr. Pearson was signing the memorandum, I was smiling from ear to ear, knowing that God's grace surely was shining upon Lawrence Academy.

In amazement, I asked, "Mr. Pearson, what made you come down here?"

"My wife, Lula asked me to come down here and see if there was anything that I could do. And here I am."

As we were chatting, Dr. McGuire faxed the memorandum to the charter school office. "Mr. Pearson, I have always admired you, and now I admire you even more. There aren't many dedicated educators today. My mother talked about you all the time. She was eventually the principal at Ethel Beckford Elementary School," Dr. McGuire said.

"Oh wow, I knew your mother very well, he said. "I was sorry to hear about her passing away. Your mother didn't play. You didn't hear about any problems at her school. When students came to her school, they knew she was about business. I guess that is why both of us are present to help this little girl, here."

It was great to think of Mr. Pearson seeing me as a little girl when actually I was forty plus. He had been in education over forty years. "Well, I can't thank both of you enough, and I guarantee you that Lawrence Academy is going to be a success," I said as I embraced both of them individually.

As Dr. McGuire was about to exit, she said, "Well, I have to go now, and I will see you bright and early on Monday morning. You have a lot of work to do." Mr. Pearson and I escorted Dr. McGuire to her car. We found Jerome, who let us in the building. He gave me a key and assured me he would be around if I needed him.

I knew this would have been a proud moment for mom. Lawrence Academy was named in the memory of my mother, Roxie Lawrence, and in the honor of my father, Allen Lawrence. My father was now elderly, but still living independently with the assistance of my brother, Joseph. Even though they only had twelve years of education between the two of them, my parents had vision and fortitude to recognize the importance of instilling core values in their eight children. It is evident that my background laid the foundation of Lawrence Academy which focuses on character education. The passing away of my mother in 2004 had given me the impetus to write the application for the school and see it through for approval by Miami-Dade School Board on April 13, 2005. Maybe it was a midlife crisis, but I knew I wanted to help students that had the greatest need. I always felt that my generation was the generation of hope, and I was one of the recipients of many of the programs that came about as a result of the 1960s civil rights movement. Now, I just wanted to give back a little that was given to me.

The death of my mother made me realize that she had given her life to her family and inner circle. She was perhaps one of the wisest persons I knew, and her quiet strength was evident. My father was traditional in that he ruled his home with an iron fist, but the needs of his family were met. One of the most memorable childhood memories was my father building a puppet stage for my social studies presentation that would accommodate several children. I used one of mommy's old curtains to encase the bottom. My group received an "A," and it made me proud of what my father had done.

Bringing me back to reality, Mr. Pearson asked me where I planned on getting some desks. There were already some office desks that were left there which could be used as teacher desks and the science desks that had been ordered had arrived.

I knew my former principal was getting new desks for her school. I called her. Ms. Leal was more than willing to help. Within fifteen minutes, I had put together a plan for two of Jerome's handymen to pick up 60 desks on Saturday morning for a modest fee. I was scheduled to pick up the U-Haul truck early Saturday morning. I also called some of my parents to come out and help as well. The three teachers and the registrar that I had hired were happy to learn that we were opening on Monday. It was great having Sandy, a registrar whom I had known at a previous school, to help me schedule students into classes until my new registrar was trained.

I knew that Mr. Pearson would not be able to help me on Saturday, but I was grateful for his guidance throughout the process. He had been on dialysis for the previous year. Initially, I would not have dreamed of approaching him to help me, but his daughter, Kathy, who was a good friend of mine, told me that her father was the ideal person to help me get started, and indeed he was.

Long after Mr. Pearson had left, I lingered around, writing down copious notes detailing everything I needed to do. I was simultaneously excited and exhausted, if that is possible. Before I realized, it was approaching six o'clock, and I had to pick up my kids from Ms. Pam, a home daycare that many working moms entrusted with their precious little cargo. I picked them up and headed straight to *Get Smart* to buy some items to decorate the school. I called my husband, Michael, to let him know I had picked up the kids and that we would be home around 9:00 p.m. Since it was so late, I picked a pasta dish and the trimmings from the Italian restaurant next door to *Get Smart*. Little Michael was asleep before we arrived home and Melanie was entertaining me with our favorite song that we had composed, "*I Love Pizza*."

As I was calling Michael, I noticed the (305) 995-1000 missed call, and I immediately clicked on the number to receive the message "This is Ms. Wardell from Charter School Office to inform you that Lawrence Academy will not open on Monday, August 8th because a fire permit and a certificate of occupancy has not been received." I knew it wasn't true because a small miracle had happened that day.

On the following day, Michael and I took the kids with us to pick up the truck, and he drove the truck to the building. There were many people waiting for us when we arrived. While Jerome's handymen went to pick up the desks, Michael and a couple of parents put the science desks together.

Ms. Stevenson, one of the teachers, along with several parents, began decorating the school. She was a person of a few words, but she was an efficient worker. Her resume indicated that she graduated in the top 5 percent of her class at Southridge Senior High. Her father was a colleague of mine for years. We gave our kids some activities to work on while we began organizing everything. Ms. Stevenson had quite a few things of her own. Both of her parents were educators, and they had given her all the basic materials needed to decorate a science and math class. There were four rooms: math and science, language arts and reading, social studies and technology, and a tutorial classroom. Everything was shaping up nicely. Finally, we raised a big welcome sign in the reception area.

Our handymen arrived and placed twenty desks in each classroom. The science desks were temporarily placed in the social studies and technology room since it was the largest. It was well past 1:00 p.m. and I ordered pizza for everyone. Two additional teachers, Ms. LaCount and Mr. Casteel arrived to get their classrooms organized. Ms. LaCount was full-figured with a motherly demeanor and Mr. Casteel was clean-cut with a slight build. I could not believe how everything was falling into place.

Ms. Stevenson's fiancé helped me to return the truck. Afterwards, there was not much that needed to be done, except I had to go to Office Depot to print the Opening of School information and the Student Handbooks.

Michael took Melanie to school for her first day as a first grader, and I took Michael to Ms. Pam at 6:30 a.m., so that I could arrive by 7:00 a.m. There was no one there when I arrived. I opened the door and placed all the opening-of-school materials on each of the teachers' desk. I was nervous, but confident that everything would go well. Slowly, the teachers arrived, and the students began to arrive. The students looked nice in their blue and white uniforms and ties. As the students trickled in, Ms. Joseph, the registrar, directed the students to their classes. Jerome stopped by to make sure that everything was working, and the lunch vendor stopped by to get the student count.

Mr. Pearson and Mr. Stinson, our principal, arrived at about the same time. They walked around, greeting the students and making sure everything was orderly. Dr. McGuire arrived early, as she had promised, with a charter school administrator to oversee the opening of the school. We chatted briefly before she left, and she shared with me that she was assigned to oversee Lawrence Academy. Lawrence was her maiden name. I truly believe God has a sense of humor.

From the first day that we opened with sixty-three sixth and seventh graders, Lawrence Academy experienced its share of both successes and setbacks along the way. Over the years, Lawrence Academy, Inc. gained two additional charters, serving grades 9-12 in 2007 and grades K-5 in 2008. We eventually learned that commitment to serving a disadvantaged population with the determination to give all students a chance to succeed would prove challenging.

# Quest for Academic Excellence (An Overview)

Lawrence Academy Middle School received a "C" for the first year. When the educational gains for the FCAT are examined, this is impressive. With a population of seventy-six students, ninety-percent of the 6th and 7th grade students showed gains in reading and eighty percent showed gains in math. Outside of standardized testing, Lawrence Academy students participated in the United Way Campaign, advanced to the semi-finals in the Black History and Culture Brain Bowl, and were granted nine awards in the Youth Fair Exhibits.

During the third year of operation, Lawrence Academy Middle took a setback when the school received a failing grade. In spite of the failing grade, Lawrence Academy opened its doors to fifteen ninth grade high school students. It was critical for Lawrence Academy during the 2007-2008 school to get back on the right track. By affirming our mission and goals, the governing board and I embraced professional development for administration and teachers, systematic assessments for students, data analysis and re-assessments focus calendar, tutorials, science and, writing clinics, mini-lessons, and feedback. Lawrence Academy students continued to support the United Way Campaign, and, for the first time, they raised money for St. Jude's Hospital for children with cancer. With the assistance of Mr. Katz and Mr. Burnett, seven of our students organized the Lawrence Academy Boy Scout Troop 289. Additionally, thirty-eight students participated in the Youth Fair. Students also participated in the Martin Luther King Parade; they organized a Hispanic Heritage Program, student government, yearbook committee, and a newspaper committee.

With a commitment to family involvement, Lawrence Academy continued to provide activities that encouraged family involvement such as Family Day, Family Night, parental workshops, and parent booster clubs. Our quest for academic excellence and parental involvement resulted in Lawrence Academy Middle receiving a high "C" for the 2007-2008 school year, missing the "B" by only three points.

The following year, Lawrence Academy Middle received a high "B" during the 2008-2009 school year. Lawrence Academy (6-12) also became the first charter school to be accredited by Southern Association of Colleges and Schools in the Florida City/Homestead area. Thereafter, with a continuous change in grading, Lawrence Academy would have grades ranging from a "B" to a "D" from 2009 to the 2011. The major changes in grading were related to defining the raising of cutoff scores required for reading and math proficiency, increasing the standards for writing, and using the scores of the special needs populations. It was clear, that it had taken time for students to acclimate to increased standards. With a unique at-risk population primarily comes a migrant background. This presents compelling evidence suggesting that an accurate academic picture of the students' academic progress is difficult to determine.

Founded in 2007, Lawrence Academy Senior received "C" the first year and did not receive a grade for two years because of the small number in each cohort group; however, based on data, Lawrence Academy Senior would have received a "C" for both years. As Lawrence Academy Middle, Lawrence Academy Senior High's grade dropped initially with the increased standards, but rebounded after two years. The events that would drive Lawrence Academy, Inc. in many instances, was driven more by a pursuit of trying to prove its creditability rather than building on its success of turning students around. Lawrence Academy Elementary was the school to bring us to the day of reckoning on July 16, 2011.

## July 16, 2011
## (A Day of Reckoning at the District Office)

The floodgates of thoughts and memories that brought us to this point all but vanished as I heard the Director from the Charter School Operation say, "Dr. Burnett, we are ready for your school at this time." The meeting I was about to attend could erase my years of work to create an authentic community school.

At the conference room table with Directors, the Lawrence Academy supporters sat in the following order; Althea King, governing board chair; myself; Michael Burnett, my husband; Mr. Salgado, CEO of EnFamilia; Dr. Middlebrooks, administrator; Mr. Cruz, third grade math teacher; Ms. Clayton, third grade language arts teacher; Ileana Valdes, proposed administrator for the upcoming year. We also had the support of one of our most dedicated parents, Mr. and Mrs. Santana who sat in the chairs along the wall.

The Executive Director of Charter School Operations spoke first, "As you know, this meeting is to address the double 'F' of Lawrence Academy Elementary Charter School. We would like to begin the meeting by allowing you to first introduce yourself along with your position or role for this meeting with introductions. I am the Executive Director of Charter School Operations and I am a non-voting member," she said.

Following the introductions, Mr. Cruz presented a short video of Lawrence Academy depicting the founding students followed by various mini-interviews detailing the journey of Lawrence Academy from its sixty-three middle school students to the project of building a new facility.

After the video, I presented data to show that even though it appeared that students were not doing well overall, the students had made significant progress after three years.

"The six graders that were from the elementary had tremendous gains, and we presented the data in chart form. Additionally, we shared that Lawrence Academy was set up to service the community and not exclude students based on academic performance and behavior. We had experienced some success with the middle and high school students. We had welcomed elementary students from two surrounding failing charter schools. In the midst of these and other challenges, the standards for the FCAT changed every year since the elementary was tested. The first year, the minimum number of students for each grade for testing was reduced to ten. This of course, caught us by surprise, simply because this is not statistically sound. Measuring academic achievement based on a cohort of less than twenty-five students will be skewed positively or negatively. In our case, negatively skewed. The second year, the requirements increased. We had seen growth in our students, but the shift in standards proved challenging.

It was part of the inherent fiber built into the foundation of Lawrence Academy to handle the educational issues that plagued the community as professionally and honestly as we could. Within five miles of Lawrence Academy, a charter school with a similar population was handling legal issues related to "testing irregularities" and "selective enrollment." Two other nearby charter schools had closed, and the surrounding traditional schools were borderline failing. With our population, studies had shown that significant change related to standardized testing could take five to ten years since we co-opted surrounding failing schools and failing communities.

During the review Ms. Coleman, the education specialist, faulted the school for not completing the monitoring plan. Additionally, she criticized the limited amount of time that students used Reading Plus, and stated that the bi-weekly data assessments were not consistently completed. Dr. Middlebrooks, who was responsible for the interim data responded that the progress monitoring plans were, in fact completed. Dr. Middlebrooks pointed out that since Reading Plus was a supplementary program, it was difficult to implement because many of the Lawrence Academy students did not have internet access at home and as part of the annual charter school review, it was recommended for this program not to be used during the school day.

Michael, my husband, talked about the time, effort, and resources that it took to open the school. Ms. King, the governing board chair echoed his sentiment. Ms. Clayton and Mr. Cruz, both third grade teachers, highlighted some of the issues they had encountered as teachers and how they were effectively handled by the governing board and the administration.

Ms. Valdes, our new administrator for the elementary, with extensive administration experience with accountability schools outlined the action plan for the 2011-2012 school year. I had worked with Ms. Valdes, and I personally recruited her because she was not only a task-master, but had a compassion for our population of students.

Mr. Salgado, CEO of EnFamilia, Inc. a nonprofit organization that provides educational programs for a large population of migrant farm workers and low-income families living in deep South Miami Dade, spoke of the long-term partnership that Lawrence had with their organization to implement a substantive program by taking more of a community approach to education.

The committee voted unanimously to allow Lawrence Academy to remain open for another year with the condition that we accept a new contract for four years instead of the original ten years. The ten-year contract would be reinstated, contingent upon the satisfactory scores on the spring 2012 FCAT. 2.0. Ms. King accepted the proposal on the behalf of the governing board. Everyone was elated, and many members of the committee congratulated us and expressed their admiration for our commitment to the Florida City community.

# PART I
# (Wisdom and Strength)

# 2011: August 1-7
## (Time for Reflection)

The first week of August was a time of reflection for me. I was glad to find out that the summer camp our students attended at a local elementary school, sponsored by the 21st Century Learning Grant, was a success. In addition to the core curriculum, the students enjoyed arts and crafts, fieldtrips, music, games and computers. We required all of our level 1 and level 2 students in reading and math to attend. Nearly 70 percent of our students attended, and I was pleased. I would have preferred our students to have been housed at their school, but it was not due to a lack of trying. I had applied for the 21st Century Grant through the district, but I never pursued what issues or shortcomings that may have been in the proposal because there were so many issues that needed to be addressed at hand. It was strange that I never received a formal letter in regard to the outcome. There were always questions in my mind, but I had to move forward on other concerns.

I knew I could not successfully address all the issues our students were confronted with alone, and that was the primary reason I invested time and energy into helping with the development of the Florida City Children's Initiative. The committee, consisting of the Mayor, non-profit leaders, and college representatives, met on a regular basis during the spring and summer to secure the Promise Neighborhood grant. I knew that if this grant was successful, it could truly make a difference for the children in Florida City. I had reached out to the churches unsuccessfully in an effort to galvanize support in the community. The one minister who was promising retired and moved to Georgia. With the turn in the economy in 2008, our parental support decreased even more, and the stories echoed by our community involvement specialist could make the ablest man weep. Ms. Scott and our teachers filled in the gap with academic, financial, and moral support more than I could imagine.

I had always been a "big picture" theorist of education that fell in line with Dennis Littky's views. Dennis Littky is nationally known for his more than thirty-five years of innovative leadership in middle and secondary education. In his book, "*The Big Picture*" Dennis Littky points out that each of us live an average of just seventy years and we spend only 9 percent of our lives in school. Based on this theory, the only really substantial thing education can do is help us to become continuous, lifelong learners. These are learners who learn without textbooks and tests, without certified teachers and standardized curricula. The problem is getting students to love learning in the neighborhood where they live. There is no natural instinct to love learning when basic needs are not being met in the household. This propelled me on a daily basis to try to get additional support for my students by working on the Florida City Children's Initiative and other community efforts.

Lawrence Academy, Inc. had expanded to include elementary aged students in 2008 with only thirty-six students, one kindergarten and one combination first and second grade class. During the 2009 school year, Lawrence Academy's population grew from thirty-six students, to over 130 students, and by 2010, there were nearly 160 students. The percent of students receiving free and reduced lunch never went below 95 percent. Lawrence Academy welcomed most of the neighboring closed charter schools' upper elementary students. We had success from our middle school in increasing learning gains, and the percentage of students reaching proficiency, but only over time. We always provided our students with the latest state-adopted textbooks, computer access, research-based computer programs, hundreds of scholastic books, and bi-weekly tutoring. Even though we had some inexperienced teachers, we made sure that they received relevant professional development and support. We had fostered a small family-oriented environment. According to our in-house survey for accreditation, we found out that nearly 60 percent of the elementary students were related to students in the middle and/or high school. The failure of one of the schools, could adversely affect the enrollment of another. Additionally, in a 2009 parent survey, 45 percent of the elementary students had not been enrolled in a pre-school program such as Head Start or in pre-kindergarten program, which had been posing a problem for Lawrence Academy.

A major change in accountability occurred during the 2009-2010 school year. The population size for each grade level group dropped from 29 to 10. None of the accountability grades were Lawrence Academy's original students. The first group of Lawrence Academy students would be the 3rd grade students for 2011-2012 school year. The students who adversely affected the school grade during the 2009-2010 FCAT, however, had made significant gains in reading (55%) and in math (85%). *Even though Lawrence's Academy's true success would reveal itself with the 3rd graders, we would be held accountable for a group that were not included in our plans.*

Beyond school, I had the same issues and concerns as any working wife and mother, such as what nutritious meals I should prepare, or how I could ensure that my children's homework was complete. I was getting home late on a regular basis. My husband and I decided to let Michael, our son, who had been a student at Lawrence Academy Elementary since kindergarten, to attend our neighborhood school as a result of all of the long and unpredictable hours I was spending at the school. Even though Michael adjusted well to the school, he was exhausted when he had to stay with me after school on a regular basis. Melanie had been at the same school since the first grade and she blossomed into a mature sixth grader. Neither my husband nor I had immediate family members to assist us in the raising of our children, so we heavily relied on each other to make sure their needs were being met. With the late hours and seemingly endless paper trail, I considered closing Lawrence Academy and returning to Miami-Dade County Public Schools, but every time I would get discouraged, a little voice inside of me would always say that giving up is not an option and almost simultaneously my husband would encourage me to "hang in there."

One of those late days was the governing board meeting held on August 4th. The meeting, called to order at 6:32 p.m., was attended by Ileana Valdes, Toni Fuller, Ken Cooper, Lucy Santamaria, and Althea King. I formally introduced Ileana as the new principal of the elementary school. The major area of discussion was related to the opening of the school and the accountability requirements related to the elementary school. We had concerns about our attorney. He had come highly recommended to us and his resume was impressive, showing he had worked extensively with charter schools. We were all taken aback when he admitted he had dropped the ball on several major issues relating to our lease. Nevertheless, the damage had been done, and we needed to move on. We were in the market for a new attorney. We also had to consider staff/cost reduction to offset the cost of our move and the investment of new equipment in the new building. After a lengthy discussion, our meeting adjourned at 8:23 p.m. and the next meeting was scheduled for September 22nd.

Ms. King had surprised me with a birthday cake, and I was humbled when everyone wished me a belated birthday. We chatted and laughed about small matters after the meeting to lighten the mood.

## 2011: August 8-14
## (Teacher Preparation Surpasses Lease Issues)

The Charter School Review Board finally had approved our move into our new facility and there was quite a bit of moving to do. Mr. Rondon, our Human Resource clerk, did an excellent job of securing all the permits that were needed to open at our new site. There were relevant issues that were raised in the meeting about the move, but the issues relating to the elementary school overshadowed everything. Placing such a major responsibility on our attorney to negotiate our lease appeared to be a major mistake, but in reality, it was not. Lawrence Academy's Governing Board made the best decision based on several recommendations, and on his credentials. I reflected on a statement from the late Dr. Ralph Lewis, our second Governing Board Chair and former Florida International University professor and special assistant to Superintendent Merrett Stierheim during his administration. Dr. Lewis stated that a good lease must have an "out," and with the investment we had made, an "out" was feasible.

What were the issues with the lease? Two years prior to our commitment to the current lease, our governing board was approached by a local real estate developer in South Florida who had built two charter schools in Broward. He had proposed building two state of the art facilities on a nearby site. It was proposed that one of the buildings could be built immediately, while the second one could be built as the school population grew. The building was exactly what we needed, but the price was too steep in our estimation. We needed legal advice to guide us through the negotiation process, and that is where our attorney failed us. We had to move forward, and the most important thing at the time was to have the school ready by August 22nd. The facility housed 30,000 ample square feet of space, including a library, computer lab, and twenty-seven moderately-sized class rooms.

George, our handyman, along with his crew, successfully transferred the furniture and equipment to the new building. In spite of Michael's pressing schedule, he made it to the school after work every day to help George with the move and to ensure everything was in place. On one of the mornings when I assisted George with our move, a snake was directly in front the entrance and as George got closer to him, the snake struck out at him. In his attempt to kill the snake with one of his nearby tools, the snake slithered away. What a way to be greeted at our new facility!! From the biblical stories to the countless stories that my mother shared with me, snakes were always an omen of evil. I could not erase from my mind the possibility that we had made a grave mistake in moving.

We had to proceed with our plan of action. School was set to begin on August 22nd, and we had our work cut out for us. Ms. Valdes was a hard worker, very organized and genuine about helping the community. The teachers reported early for detailed professional development meetings planned carefully to meet every possible need of the teachers from August 8th - 14th including professional responsibilities and differentiated accountability requirements. Everything was scheduled into the old facility during the transition to the new facility. We welcomed Ms. King, who reviewed the goals and expectations, followed by Ms. Valdes' review of the differentiated accountability requirements for 2011-2012. Mr. Katz followed with the data analysis, with a recap of 2011 school grade, test design summary, and the individual academic improvement plan for each student. The remaining days included such topics as Webb's Depth of Knowledge, school-wide reading and writing initiatives, course content reading and writing, explicit instruction, lesson planning, use of pacing guides, instructional focus calendars, review of the Next Generation Sunshine State Standards, classroom culture of learning, classroom management, class expectations, and course syllabi, data chats, use of rubrics and informal and formal assessments. The administrative staff supplied not only physical materials and supplies, but also a community of psychological support.

Ms. Scott, our community involvement specialist, scheduled a Parent Task Force meeting on August 2nd. At the school meeting, she discussed the change to the new school, summer packets, and fundraising efforts. The orientation meeting for parents was held on August 13th. The principals were introduced, and they briefly spoke and introduced the teachers. I gave the vision and mission of the school, and Ms. Scott presented a Title I presentation and covered the school compact. The floor was open for suggestions, and one parent commented that she would like to have select dates that parents could see teachers outside of the open house night. Ms. Scott informed her that Lawrence Academy always had "Family Nite," generally scheduled the last Friday of each month, for parents, teachers, and administrators. They were granted the opportunity to attend a program with food and activities.

## 2011: August 15-21 (Classroom Preparation)

The third week of August was as busy as ever. Most of everything was in place, the teachers had begun to decorate their rooms and prepare their lesson plans. Everyone appeared to be in good spirits and excited about the building. There was an opening-of-school meeting on August 18th for all teachers. Ileana distributed the opening of school packet and reviewed the procedures. An equipment form was given to teachers to identify any equipment or books that they might need, and the fire drill procedures were covered since there had to be a fire drill the first week of school. Collecting the school fee had been difficult because ninety-nine percent of the students received free or reduced lunch; therefore, the school fee had been reduced from $45.00 to $35.00, which included the t-shirt, student ID, science fee, and student agenda.

Ms. Valdes and I established our late afternoon chat to debrief. I was happy to learn that she had hired a full-time ESE/ELL specialist that had been a special education teacher for nearly ten years at the district and was working on her doctorate in the field. Ms. Valdes and I strongly believed that she could handle the paper trail and provide support to the teachers. Ms. Steele, one of our new and enthusiastic teachers, had begun to show positive signs that she would be a career teacher who was eager to have everything perfect for her students every day. She quickly became one of the dedicated teachers that I could guarantee would be in her classroom late after school, preparing her lessons. On many occasions I saw her "devotion" to perfection; it encouraged my heart more than she would ever know.

## 2011: August 22-31 (Beginning of School!!!)

The anticipation of the first day of school was exciting. This was the first day Lawrence Academy would be in their new state of the art building. I was up by 4:00 a.m., but I did not leave until 7:30 a.m. to drop off my kids to school. This was the beginning of my morning routine for the 2011-2012 school year. I had informed Mr. Katz and Ms. Valdes that my arrival time would be between 8:30 a.m. and 9:00 a.m. each day. Before I left for work, I would check my e-mails, complete any documents that needed my attention, make breakfast, shower and dress.

When I arrived at school, everyone was in class. Since we had access to the former facility until the last day of August, to reduce traffic, the new enrollees were directed to report to the old facility. Mr. Katz informed me that a representative from the CSO had sent someone to check on the move to the new building, and they were pleased with the transition.

Overall, the first day of school was a success. At dismissal, the teachers, as well as our security, stood outside. I saw a little bit of commotion on the side of the building, so I moved hurriedly in that direction. A parent was upset because she had instructed her two sons to stay after school until she picked them up, but according to their teacher, they stated that they were to walk home. I explained to the parent that until the "back to school" documents are returned, we rely on what the students tell us. I assured her that everything was going to be all right.

Ms. Lara, the reading coach, who was nearby chimed in words of comfort. To soothe the parent's state of panic, we volunteered to ride home with her to make sure everything was alright. As soon as Ms. Lara and I could get in the SUV, the frantic parent started driving recklessly in the direction of her home. I glanced at Ms. Lara. "Ms. …., "I said. "I know you are upset, and you have every right to be at this time," I interjected between her moments of panic, "but we are not going to do anyone any….good if we don't arrive safely."

I guess the entire ride was probably three minutes at most, but it felt like an eternity. Standing on grass, in front of a moderately built home, were both of her adorable boys. "Why didn't you stay until I picked you up?" the mother asked. They shrugged their shoulders, and eventually the older one said, "I thought you wanted us to walk home."

"What is important, is that both of you are safe," Ms. Lara reassured the parent and the students.

"I will make sure that both of their teachers know that they are to wait for you," I emphasized and if it changes, please send a note." The parent drove us back to the school, and she thanked us for our concern, but I had to think, "Was this the second omen of the year that would take us all for a ride?"

After my nerves had settled down a bit, I went to Ms. Valdes' office to recap the day, which would become part my daily routine. After giving her a rundown of Ms. Lara's and my brief, but intense little escapade, we quickly turned our attention to business with our plan of action for the elementary. I reviewed the daily intervention schedule for math and reading, and the proposed tutorials. I agreed that we would rotate the afterschool and Saturday tutorial sessions so that neither one of us would burn out. The partnership that Ms. Valdes and I had at a local school together was one of the main reasons we respected each other as professionals. Both of us were dedicated, hard workers, and most of all, we valued integrity.

## 2011: September 1-11 (The Leadership Team)

September 1st was the date of our first Leadership Team meeting of the year. I was expecting this meeting to be long and productive. The items on the agenda were divided by curriculum and operations. The meeting was called to order by the Governing Board Chairperson, Ms. Althea King. The following individuals were present: Israel Katz, Ileana Valdes, Thomas Dunn (Dean of Students), Aimee Lara, Eva Grambling (ESE/ELL Chairperson) and I. The first item on the agenda was the checklist for the state visit. It was a lengthy list. We were able to assign tasks to individual team members to ensure everything would be ready for September 12th. Ms. Lara stated that she would assist Ms. Valdes and the teachers with the data charts scheduled on September 7th and September 8th. Mr. Katz and I agreed to help Ms. Valdes with the review of the textbooks and software, general walkthroughs and lesson plan checklist feedback. Ms. Grambling stated she had prepared the ELL and SPED letters intended for all parents.

Reviewing the checklist and assigning tasks for the state visit took nearly two hours. Mr. Katz dismissed himself to the cafeteria for the elementary lunch. We continued with the meeting and discussed the dates for "back to school nite" scheduled for Wednesday, September 21st for the elementary and October 5th for the middle and high school. I insisted that in spite of the state visit and the elementary school sanctions, we had to keep some sense of normalcy, and everyone agreed. I informed the team that student elections, as well as Hispanic heritage, were main events on the calendar, and we needed to make sure that the teachers incorporated lessons about voting/democracy and the contributions of Hispanics in America. At the end of day, Ms. Valdes and I met and were pleased with the progress and the sense of community.

On the days that I picked up my children from school, I would frequently receive calls from various people from the school about current issues, and I would make the calls a "guess who" game with my children.

It was Labor Day weekend. It was a relief to have a three-day holiday. After a grueling first two weeks of school, I think that I slept 2/3 of it away, and as a result, we missed our routine 11:00 a.m. service on Sunday.

On Monday, with the help of my husband, we pulled together a nice little barbecue in the back yard just for us and a movie that my husband was itching to see, Apollo 18. We had a full day, and by 9:00 p.m., the kids were in their beds while my husband and I got ready for work by checking e-mails and completing mini-tasks just to make the week go a little smoother.

We had a faculty meeting on September 6th to cover assertive discipline, the differentiated accountability visit, Individual Professional Development Plans (IPDP), ESE/ELL, insurance, the school website, and school committees. Mr. Dunn had visited the KIPP school in Jacksonville, Florida to learn more about their discipline plan. He shared his observations with the staff and his plan of discipline for the teachers. Although Mr. Dunn had a great plan, I realized it was an overwhelming amount of information for our one and half hour meeting. Ms. Valdes promised that we would revisit the plan on another day, because we had to move to the DA visit, which took the majority of the time.

On September 7th, we had our Leadership Meeting with the following items on the agenda; Response to Intervention, Curriculum Updates, and Concerns. Althea King, Israel Katz, Ileana Valdes, Thomas Dunn, Aimee Lara, Eva Grambling and I were present. The major area of discussion was response to intervention. Ms. Grambling briefed Ms. King on what response to intervention was. Ms. Valdes and Ms. Lara had designed the three-tiers of services to students that we were offering, and the list of students that fell under each tier. Part of our response to intervention plan was discipline. Mr. Dunn and Ms. Grambling volunteered to meet September 9th to work on a plan, which would include a professional development for teachers. Mr. Katz and I updated the team on the middle and high school. Under the current academic sanction of the elementary school, the middle and high schools had to take a back seat to the elementary school, which demanded the attention and time of everyone.

## 2011: September 12-18
## (The State Visit and a Jewel on the Sideline)

Florida Assessment for Instruction in Reading (FAIR) Testing was scheduled on September 12th, the day of the DA visit. The assessment system provides teachers screening, diagnostic, and progress monitoring information that is essential to guiding instruction. This was scheduled after lunch, when the State DA Team would be meeting with the leaders of the school. I was pleased that Ms. Sharon VanSmith, our part-time librarian and a personal friend, had volunteered to prepare a continental breakfast and set-up lunch for the DA team. She was a jewel.

The leader of the state visit was Ms. Gina Eyerman. I remember vividly because as she introduced herself, she acknowledged that many items such as the common board that are on checklist inventories were not necessarily the things that translate into the quality of learning that is being assessed, and that was why the format was changed.

"If you look at the agenda, we will have introductions and presentation of the self-study, conduct classroom observations, DA team working lunch, brief overview of findings, and then we will pre-arrange content teams to identify content areas of need based on our observations and the SIP Plan," stated Ms. Eyerman.

At that moment, I reflected on the e-mail that Mr. Ed Radigan from the state's Bureau of School Improvement sent me on July 16, 2008 when the middle school went from an "F" to a "C" and was within three points of making a "B." In his e-mail, he stated that "of all the schools I worked with this year, there is no doubt in my mind you and your staff were the most dedicated to improving your school. I was proud and happy to have played a small role in the school's success."

After the introductions, I gave the overview of the history of the school which included welcoming students from neighboring closed charter schools. A major change in accountability had occurred during the 2009-2010 school year. The population size for each grade went from twenty-nine to ten. We were already committed to the students we had accepted from closed charters. I believed Lawrence Academy Elementary's true potential would reveal itself with the current 3$^{rd}$ graders. This was the first group of students identified as Lawrence Academy students for the entire three years, as indicated by the FAIR data. Ms. Valdes followed my overview with the Self-Assessment of Problem Solving Implementation (SAPSI).

For the most part, Lawrence Academy Elementary was on target. The areas that were deficit were the lack of a beliefs survey to assess the level of commitment and impact of PS/RTI on faculty, emotional/behavioral disabilities, Tier 3, and a school-based leadership team with parents. Ms. Eyerman was the first to comment that she understood the challenges of getting parents in this community to participate in such a forum because of their work commitments and the belief many had that they did not have anything to offer. Shortly thereafter, the State DA team visited classrooms from 10:30 a.m.-12:00 noon, followed by lunch. Lawrence Academy purchased sandwiches from Subway, and various staff members donated drinks, chips, and cookies.

Directly after lunch, Ms. Eyerman gave a brief overview of the team's findings; she indicated that the facility and learning environment had dramatically improved. There were a few behavioral issues that they saw, but nothing that could not easily be managed by implementing a behavioral program. Ms. King observed that we had begun the process with our discipline plan spearheaded by our Dean of Students and it was our expectation to have Positive Behavior Support (PBS) implemented within a couple of weeks. Mrs. King told us that this process is a continuous process and that Lawrence Academy hoped to find the concerns identified by the self-study team and the state corrected by the February visit. Within the brief time remaining, we needed to get with our teams to identify content areas of need based on observations and the SIP Plan, review the SIP Plan, make recommended revisions/additions to the plan, and develop a draft for the next steps.

Ms. Valdes was placed on the Reading, English and Language Arts team with Mr. Carlos Rossie from the state, Ms. Pauline Ward and Dr. Monica Oliva from the district, and Ms. Aimee Lara, from Lawrence Academy. I was placed on the Mathematics team with Ms. Gayle Sitter from the state, and Ms. Teresa Diaz-Gonzalez, Ms. Patrice Baptiste, from the district. Mr. Katz was placed on the science team with Ms. Shakeatha Butler from the state, and Ms. Felicia Price from the district.

We did not discuss in detail any recommendations in under an hour because quite a bit of time was spent answering questions posed by the team members. When we left the meeting, we felt good about the progress we had made as a school, but we also began to see more of the mounting pile of issues that at times would consume us.

A Leadership Team meeting was scheduled on the 15th to review the findings from the state visit and to continue to hammer out an effective cohesive plan of action.

For simplicity sake, we compiled a six-page document of all the tasks that needed to be completed, the person responsible and the proposed date of completion. Finally, we not only had a workable document to submit to the district, but also a workable document for the school to follow.

# 2011: September 19-25
# (From Open House to Board Meeting and Everything In Between)

On September 21st, we had a respectable turn-out for the elementary school's Open House. Parents reported to the cafeteria for an overview of the history and mission of the school. Ms. Valdes highlighted the importance of parental involvement and keeping abreast of each child's academic and behavioral progress. Following the meeting, we served an arroz con pollo dinner funded by donations from parents. It seemed that food always served as a galvanizing force to get parents out and to put them at ease with the teachers to discuss the progress of their children. I enjoyed being part of the team to serve the parents and I felt they appreciated the hospitality.

The following day, September 22nd, was early release and another Leadership Team was scheduled to continue our discussion on the progress and the status of each school, which included, testing, safety and health guidelines, and the safety and discipline plans. Within the timeframe between 12:50 p.m.-1:15 p.m., we held a general meeting to discuss the items from the Leadership Team Meeting, and following, we conducted four breakout groups.

The first session, conducted by Felicia Price was the Five E's. The Five E's instructional model is based on the constructivist approach to learning which emphasizes the importance of learners building or constructing new ideas on top of their old ideas. The five E's stand for engage, explore, explain, elaborate, and evaluate. The five E's guide students and teachers to use and build upon prior knowledge and experience and to continually assess and develop their understanding of the concept. The K-2 educators and the language arts 3-5 were assigned to the guided reading session facilitated by Ms. Lara, our reading coach. The other three sessions were guided instruction, science/math instruction, and Diagnostic Assessment of Reading (D. A. R.). The math and science teachers from both the middle and high school were assigned to the math/science session facilitated by Ms. Baptiste, the math coach from the district. Dr. Middlebrooks, the language arts department chair conducted the DAR session, which all of the secondary language arts and social studies staff attended.

I stayed around late that evening because there was a governing board meeting scheduled for 6:30 p.m. Ms. King was the first to arrive, as usual. The meeting was called to order at 6:30 p.m. and the following members were present; Ms. Lucy

Santamaria, Mr. Melvin Dennis, Mr. Ken Cooper, and visiting, Mr. Tom McClary. As part of the Director's Report, I focused on the steps to improve academic performance, activities scheduled for the upcoming months, and the costs of moving to the new facility. Mr. Hunter, our accountant, was scheduled to come to the school on Monday to help me revise the budget as a result of the increased cost of services needed for the elementary school. The old business focused on the status of the elementary and the need to recruit new board members. Most of the members on the board had been on the board for over five years, and there was a need to find replacements, particularly for Ms. King. Ms. King was putting in a full-time schedule at Lawrence Academy without pay. Whenever I had the opportunity, I would shower her with gratitude. The meeting was adjourned at 8:00 p.m.

My usual stop on the way home after the Governing Board meetings was Starbucks. This allowed me to have one of my favorite drinks, a grande cappuccino with four raw sugars topped with whipped cream, before heading home. This time alone gave me a moment to reflect about my God, my family and my purpose. It always gave me a deeper appreciation of everything, regardless of the circumstances. When I arrived home around nine, it was always more than gratifying to see that everything was well. My husband did not always agree with some of my late hours, but he knew a lot was at stake. Both of us were overachievers who understood the principle of sacrifice.

## 2011: September 26-30
## (Following the Valdes Shuffle)

As usual, Ms. Valdes was on task. Ms. Valdes scheduled a coaches' meeting on September 26, 2011 to keep track of everyone's daily schedule so that overlapping would not occur. The coaches were informed that while all coaches were assigned to Lawrence Academy, our critical areas were grades 3-5 and the implementation of the common core standards specifically this year with K-1. Ms. Baptiste, the math coach, was assigned to spend 60 percent of her time with Ms. Thomas, grades 4 and 5; 20 percent with Mr. Cruz, grade 3; and 20 percent with K-2. Ms. Price, the science coach was assigned 60 percent to Ms. Thomas; 20 percent with Mr. Cruz; and 20 percent with K-2. Dr. Oliva was assigned to spend 70 percent of her time with K-2, with a major concentration with the $1^{st}$ grade for writing since these students needed extensive writing skills in 2015; 20 percent with $2^{nd}$ grade teacher, Ms. Cruz in reading and Ms. Silveira; and only 10 percent with Ms. Clayton, since she had a full time paraprofessional. Ms. Lara was told to spend 70 percent of her time with Ms. LaCount, grades 4 and 5; 20 percent with Ms. Clayton; and 10 percent concentration with K-2. Additionally, coaches were briefed on the importance of the bi-weekly assessments and assisting teachers with the appropriate strategies to help deficit students on the tested benchmarks.

The following day, a faculty meeting was held after school, primarily to update the teachers on the important upcoming events on the calendar. The teachers were briefed on the following; Edusoft PD on the $29^{th}$, Family Night on September $30^{th}$, CSO Visit on the $30^{th}$, secondary Open House on October $5^{th}$, PSAT on October $12^{th}$, FCAT retakes on October $13^{th}$, and interim assessments the week of October 17th. A less significant item on the agenda was the issue with the thermostats constantly being changed in the rooms. The problem was that the building was designed with the thermostats for the classrooms at the end of the hallways, which controlled the temperature for the rest of the classrooms. Even though it might be cool in the end rooms, the center rooms were still warm. The bottom line was that the teachers were instructed to not change the thermostat in the classrooms. The teachers were further reminded that an Edusoft workshop was scheduled on the teacher planning day, and the day could not be used as an opt day. I could hear the mumblings of dissatisfaction among the staff, but I knew they would be there the next day. We had a staff that was dependable, and Ms. Valdes and I didn't mind the mumblings. It was a healthy exercise.

September 29, 2011, Ms. Valdes and I brought continental breakfast for the teachers and facilitators. The Edusoft training started promptly at 9:00 a.m. Mr. Katz, Ms. Valdes and I, as well as several other leadership members, had been trained on August 5th. Between my working on the budget for Mr. Hunter, Ms. Valdes meeting with elementary parents to state the urgency of their child's participation in after school and Saturday tutoring, and Mr. Katz working on the computers, we were in and out of the workshop. We knew they were in good hands. The facilitators were motivated to teach them the skills needed to access and interpret the data they needed to direct their instruction.

The lunch break was scheduled from 12:00 noon to 1:00 p.m. which allowed some time for the teachers to relax. When I entered the room to ask one of the facilitators how everything was going, the report was not good. She informed me that some teachers were on their phones and computers, and some were just not paying attention. This was not only embarrassing, but unacceptable. I told her just to give me ten minutes before they returned from lunch. With the CSO scheduled the following day, it was understandable why teachers felt the need to get things done. The facilitators said they would try to wrap things up by 2:00 p.m., and the evaluations would be sent through the mail. I, of course, informed Mr. Katz and Ms. Valdes about what had occurred.

When the teachers returned, they could see on my face that something was wrong. I was standing before them, not the facilitators. "One of the facilitators was a little disturbed that many of you are on your phones, computers and some of you are just not paying attention," I told them. "I know you have a lot on your plate, but all of us do. I know that when you were interviewed, you were told about the population that we serve and the scrutiny you might be under as a result. I can tell you from personal experience that you are working five times as hard as teachers that are at high performing schools. That is a given. But it does not give you the right to disrespect those that are trying to help us. This is the end of the topic for me and I hope for you. They have made accommodations to end early so that you do have some time to do what you need to do."

In the eyes of everyone, it appeared to be a resolution, but Aristotle said it best when he said that "educating the mind without the heart is no education at all." This goes for teachers as well as students. In essence, both teachers and students can be pushed to a laundry list of things for compliance, but inwardly, if they do not embrace what is said or done, it can be worthless.

September 30, 2011, when I arrived at 9:00 a.m., I could tell from our registrar's expression, that representatives from the charter school office had arrived. I knew the meeting was in the library. I took my time placing my belongings in the office and getting a pad and pencil for notes. Two representatives for the CSO were present along with Ms. Valdes and Ms. Grambling, our ESE specialist. It didn't take long to determine that the focus was on one item on the CSO checklist, and that was the exceptional education paper trail. I would be the first to admit that exceptional education was our major weakness; that was the major reason we hired Ms. Grambling full-time; she had ten years of experience from a district school that had a major ESE program.

It didn't matter that I had completed a two-year review of the ESE students and found that the majority of the students had made significant learning gains. Being in education for the past 25+, I knew very well the importance of documentation and follow-through. As the Response-to-Invention process was being discussed, one of the CSO representatives asked Ms. Grambling whether she had clearance from downtown. Even though Ms. Grambling did not have a break in her employment and was cleared with MDCPS, she still had to be cleared for a background check by CSO since she was presently employed by us. Wow. I knew I was busted, so I took the two minute chewing out. It was a chance that I took. It didn't matter to me that Ms. Grambling did not have a break in employment, from the moment she transferred from the school system to us, since she took a leave of absence. As usual, the school system had a backlog for clearance in the beginning of the year. It had been five weeks, and she had not received clearance. Nevertheless, we had scores of people telling us what we had to do, and we needed to get it done immediately. The CSO representative ordered Ms. Grambling to leave the premises immediately. She looked at Ms. Valdes and me. I nodded, then she gathered her things and left.

The CSO representative informed us she and a colleague would visit a couple of classrooms and leave. Ms. Valdes and I were learning to shrug things off and keep moving. We went over the reading and math intervention schedule and the tutoring schedule in detail. Even though Voyager was required by the district, I personally did not like Voyager. I understood that students have to read at their level, but at the same time, students needed to be introduced to challenging text. I personally liked Read 180, which exposes students to challenging text. The results, in my estimation, would be greater in the long run.

I was sharing with one of the charter school representatives that I had been spending some time working on making sure the budget was balanced. It took me by surprise when the representative said, "If I were you, I wouldn't worry about the budget." In many instances I never understood the suggestions or comments which were made, so I just took them at face value. At times, I felt their comments could be a little off the cuff. This particular representative had come with another charter school representative the previous year just to visit. As they were about to leave, they began joking about the "erasing parties" that had occurred in Atlanta. At the time, I did not know that a nearby charter school was implicated in "irregularities" in their testing. There is no doubt that I wanted my students to do well, but not to extent of putting my faith, reputation, and the theme of character education in honor of my parents at risk.

Ms. Valdes and I worked on the tutoring schedule when they left. For the tutoring schedule, we put together three, six to seven day reading and math sessions scheduled for the fall. Additionally, a reading plus lab, science lab, and writing lab were established after school and on Saturdays for the appropriate grades. Ms. Valdes and I added the incentive that students would be rewarded with a gift card provided they attended all the scheduled sessions in a given area. Our fingers were crossed because we knew getting parents to bring them might pose a problem.

September 30, 2011, our monthly Family Night was scheduled at 6:00 p.m. The purpose of Family Night was to encourage parents to spend time with their children, and provided parents an opportunity to spend informal time with administrators and teachers to discuss issues and concerns that they might have. After giving parents a calendar update, we divided families or groups up into groups of five and gave a 100 piece puzzle to each group. The two groups that finished first were given a small token to mark their victory. It was amazing to see how diligently the groups worked together to complete the task.

Afterwards, we provided a pasta dinner, compliments of Capri Restaurant. The parents provided the bread, drinks, salads and desserts. Board games and chess were provided. Everyone seemed to appreciate the meal. We always had a faithful few parents who would volunteer for the clean-up. The event was over by 8:00 p.m.

## 2011: October 1-7
## (From Saturday School to Budgeting Meeting)

Saturday, October 1, 2011, I arrived at the school around 9:00 a.m. for the secondary students to complete their community service hours by picking up trash around the campus. Ms. Valdes arrived a little later to begin working on the materials that would be used for tutoring. Around the time the students were about to sign-out for their community service, I saw my husband, Michael, from the window drive up in the parking lot with our children, Michael and Melanie. This was always my signal to leave. This gave Melanie and me the opportunity to spend some time together while the guys were in a scouting meeting. I would use this time to do some shopping or any other errands that I had to do, but I would also use this time to dine with my daughter and catch the latest movie. If there was a party, I would be the one to take her. On occasions when there was a major project that she had to do, we stayed at the school to complete it.

My husband was faithful to the Boy Scouts, which he helped to establish at Lawrence Academy. Every Saturday, he, along with two faithful parents, would meet with the cubs and the scouts in the cafeteria. About twelve students would consistently make the meetings. They would work on projects, go on outings such as camping, fishing, and scouting jamborees. It was something that not only provided a great opportunity for our students, but it also gave my husband a sense of purpose as well. The scout leaders had begun to teach the boys to play chess. I could see our vision for Lawrence Academy materializing.

On Monday, October 3, 2011, our accountant, Mr. Hunter and Ms. Rondon, our internal accounting clerk, met with me to begin working on possible reductions in the budget to accommodate the additional cost for the services and materials for the elementary students. My philosophy is that the people at the top should take the greatest cut, and the remaining cuts should be spread equally around. I couldn't help but think that perhaps the Governing Board and I made the wrong decision to move. Even though this had been in the plans for over three years because of concerns we had about the safety of the building we were in, I felt that Murphy's Law was in motion.

In the course of the meeting, we arrived at a tentative reduction in the budget, which included an eighteen percent reduction starting with me, and a ten-day furlough for the principals between January 1st and April 15th. The dean of students, SPED specialist and counselor would serve one hour per day as interventionists. All full-time teachers would be required to take four furlough days from the following dates, December 19th, January 23rd, February 3rd, March 30th, March 15th, March 16th, June 14th, and June 15th. Four days for the support staff and part-time staff was also added. One teacher would be surplused and the art teacher would be reduced to part-time. The library would be suspended after the holidays. It was a difficult decision, but it had to be done. The proposal was now set for board approval, and what was remaining was the task of breaking the news to the staff.

October 5, 2011 was Back-to-School night for the middle and high school. It was scheduled to begin with a parent orientation starting at 6:00 p.m. There was a presentation on Title 1 in the cafeteria, with the classroom visits starting promptly at 6:30 p.m. There were more elementary school parents in attendance than were present a couple of weeks earlier at the middle and high school Back-to-School. This was not surprising since parents do support their younger children more so than the older ones. The overall attendance at our three schools was much lower than schools that I had worked previously, but I was satisfied. Mr. Katz made the Connect-Ed calls to all homes, Mrs. Valdes sent notices home with the students, and our community involvement specialist, Ms. Scott, made personal calls home two to three days in advance to remind parents of the event.

## 2011: October 8-14 (Making It Work)

On October 8, 2011, Ms. Scott was not only the Community Involvement Specialist, but also the Parent Task Force coordinator. She worked closely with Melissa, who had two children at Lawrence Academy. Their major discussions at 10:30 a.m. focused on stressing the importance of their children's attendance, completing home learning assignments, reading and attending the scheduled tutoring sessions. The Parent Task Force scheduled several fundraisers to help provide gift card incentives to students that attended all of the scheduled tutorials.

On October 11, 2011, a faculty meeting was scheduled to remind secondary teachers about the preparation and dates for the FCAT retakes, and all teachers about the upcoming fall interim. We spent about thirty minutes introducing teachers to the Village Learning website. They got the opportunity to see the supplementary activities and lessons available to them. It was amazing to see the teachers lose track of time exploring the site. It was quite different from the Edusoft workshop.

Ms. King, our Governing Board Chair, who had a degree in English, and had been a life-long educator and administrator in the system, began to volunteer her time twice a week to help the elementary school. She worked specifically with the 4th graders in reading and writing.

The seniors held a bake sale for the entire week of October 10th to begin fundraising for their senior activities. They were selling pizza and items for the sweet tooth, and raking in an average of $40.00 a day, which was a great start. Becky unofficially took the leadership role as President until the official student government elections. She wanted to make the Class of 2012 senior year special. Becky and most of her classmates had started Lawrence Academy six years previously, and they would be graduating June 8th at the South Dade Cultural Arts Center.

On October 14th, I had a meeting with the teachers who were the recipients of the 2011-2012 MAP funds based on their performance and student test scores. The MAP funds were specifically earmarked to reward charter school teachers for exemplary performance. The recipients were Ms. Grissella Cruz, Ms. Sheneka Stevenson, Ms. Jose Cruz, and Ms. Ariana Blandon.

## 2011: October 15-21
## (Balancing Family, Lawrence Academy Elementary, Lawrence Middle, and Lawrence Academy Senior)

October 15, 2011, the Cub Scouts had their first outing to the annual Jurassic Park Outing. This was an opportunity for the scouts to learn various survival skills, from tying a knot to making a campsite. Some of the scouts received badges for completing the requirements. The students were so proud of their accomplishments. We decided to start allowing the students to wear their Boy Scout uniforms on Tuesdays.

Regardless of whatever was going on with Lawrence Academy, Michael and I always made sure that special events were celebrated. Our daughter, Melanie's, birthday was on the 19th, but we celebrated her birthday after church on the 16th with her favorite pasta and shrimp dinner. As long as I could remember, Melanie had always loved shrimp and pasta. Perhaps I had marked her at birth because seafood and pasta was my favorite as well. Her godparents, Diann and William joined the celebration with gifts.

October 17, 2011, the interim assessments commenced and continued throughout the week. Ms. Valdes worked with the coaches and teachers to administer the assessments. She was eager to see what the results would be over the baselines and set up an intervention plan based on the results.

We also had our first incidence of vandalism, and Mr. Katz was livid. A student punched a hole in the wall on the elementary floor, but one of the elementary students witnessed and reported a high school student that was on the floor during that time. The students had finally found out that we did not have the secret cameras that we said we had. The camera system we had in the old facility could not be used in the new facility. The stairwells had no source of electricity. It would have been very expensive to run the wires. The installation was placed on hold, and we used high school student monitors to prevent vandalism. The founding students were particularly protective of the new facility. Mr. Katz could not extend the full extent of the penalty to the student for vandalism because the younger student only witnessed him leaving the scene.

October 19, 2011, Ms. Scott and I took twelve of our seniors to College Day, held at Sweet Home Missionary Church where nearly thirty colleges and universities around the country convened to accept students on the spot with scholarships. With resumes and transcripts in hand, students filled out applications and talked to college recruiters. Some students received scholarship offers from small colleges in other states. Even though I joined in the happiness of their prospects, I knew that the cost of travel would be a hindrance. We made sure that the local colleges would be part of their plan by inviting them to the school.

Directly after the college event, Ms. Scott and I took the students to a nearby fast food restaurant. It was always nice after these types of events to be with the students in a non-school setting. In all my years as an educator, it never failed that students were more likely to discuss their immediate issues and concerns, as well as share their inner most thoughts about their dreams and aspirations, in a different venue. This information was valuable in getting the students the "real type" of support they needed. Ms. Scott identified a list of public and private agencies that might provide assistance to students for economic, emotional, and personal support.

After school, Ms. Valdes met with the elementary teachers to introduce Brainchild and the proposed intervention schedule. She informed them that she applied for an intervention tutoring grant for the ESOL population and she had individual data chats with teachers. Monday, October 24th, the teachers were scheduled to begin their data chats with the students.

On the evening of October 19th, EnFamilia, a nonprofit agency established in 2000 by Carlos and Rocio Salgado provided educational programs to help to improve and preserve family life for a large population of migrant farm workers and low-income families living deep in South Miami-Dade County in partnerships with the Parent Academy, Miami-Dade County Schools, and the World's Greatest Dads. They sponsored a series of eight workshops entitled: "Promoting Responsible Fatherhood" at Lawrence Academy. It was to take place twice a week. My husband was one of the facilitators who led the English speaking workshops. He had received the training and certification in Washington, DC. Michael had six men who attended the workshops. Mr. Salgado and his brother were facilitators for the Spanish-speaking workshops; fifteen men regularly attended. These workshops were designed to help our fathers become more supportive of children who would be instrumental in helping our students to succeed. This was a major step we took to help build stronger families.

The eight topics were: The Roots of Fathering, Fathering "The Little Boy Within", The Power To Meet My Own Needs,

Overcoming Barriers to Nurturing Fathering: Anger, Alcohol/ Other Substances, and Stress, Discipline, A Time and Place for Fathering, Healing the Father Wound. EnFamilia provided dinner for everyone as well as babysitting. This provided extra income for our paraprofessionals and Winn-Dixie gift cards for all participants.

October 20, 2011, the governing board met to discuss the update of the facility, the status of the elementary school, recruitment of board members, Founder's Day, security of building, reimbursement for mileage, and the Governing Board on-line training. The proposed budget reduction was tabled until the December 8th meeting, after the board had the opportunity to review it. Ms. Valdes presented the intervention program and schedule, and the interim results change since the baseline. The interim assessments showed a 2 percent decrease in 3rd grade reading, 18 percent increase in 4th grade reading, and a 2 percent decrease in 5th grade reading; there was an 18 percent increase in 3rd grade math, 24 percent increase in 4th grade math, 15 percent increase in 5th grade math and a 4 percent decrease in science. Overall, we were pleased with data to support the fact that our intervention program and schedule were making a significant difference. For the decrease in reading, Ms. Valdes had already begun to put a comprehensive plan together, included but not limited to direct instruction, push-ins, web-based programs, and tutorials.

On October 21st, we had our K-5 Fall Festival held after school from 4 p.m.-7:00 p.m. We had a dance with a DJ, refreshments in the cafeteria, and outside activities. The kids enjoyed having Mr. Katz on the dunk tank. The secondary students' dance was well attended from 7 p.m.-11 p.m. Two male parents served as volunteer security monitors.

## 2011: October 22-28 (Red Ribbon Week Infused with Writing and Data Chats)

October 24th marked Red Ribbon Week. In honor of Red Ribbon Week, we scheduled an Anti-Drug Pep Rally in the cafeteria, one in the morning for the elementary, and another in the afternoon for the middle and high school. A college recruiter from Washington University in Saint Louis, Missouri, was scheduled to talk to our students at noon in spite of my reservations that our students would probably not attend because of the costs associated with the distance and the strong family bonds among Hispanics that discouraged them from moving far away from home.

This was also the week we had scheduled Writing Across the Curriculum with the topic of Drug Awareness. In the secondary schools, a student might write an essay using the six traits of writing in science on the chemistry of drugs, while in language arts they might write a personal account of someone they know who has struggled with drug addiction.

Ms. Valdes met with the coaches on the 25th to discuss the interim results, data chats and interventions.

The faculty meeting scheduled on October 25th was cancelled because of early release on October 27th. The time was used to update everyone on our progress, and provided a time for common planning for language arts/social studies with Dr. Middlebrooks as the facilitator, and math/science with Ms. Blandon as the facilitator.

On October 28th, grades were due for the first grading period. We told the teachers that after their grades were complete, they could leave for a long lunch. I completed the Capital Outlay plans to obtain funds that were reserved to cover capital expenses for charter schools that were also due for the middle and high schools. The elementary school did not qualify as a result of the school grade which was one of the contributing factors in our budget.

# 2011: October 29-31
# (Intervention Program and Phase 1
# of Saturday Academy)

The elementary intervention programs were rigorous. In addition to the ninety daily minutes of reading, sixty daily minutes of math, thirty daily minutes of science and thirty daily minutes of writing, there was skill-building with *Voyager, Go Math, Buckle Down* and *FCAT Explorer*, and writing in art classes. Beginning the 26th of October, students were pulled out of art, music, PE or Social Studies for reading, math, and science. Third grade students had already begun attending the Reading Plus lab on Monday and Wednesday and the 4th and 5th graders were scheduled on Tuesday and Thursday.

Phase I of the Saturday Academy started October 29th for grades 3-5 in reading, mathematics, science and writing from 9:00 a.m.-1:00 p.m. Ms. Valdes and I were on hand there for the first Saturday Academy to cheer the students on. We had them meet in the cafeteria where they were picked up by their teacher. Eventually, we found out that we needed to serve breakfast because many of them did not have breakfast before they left home. We had plenty of cereal, milk, and fruit that we began to serve in addition to a nutritious afternoon snack. Ms. Valdes reminded the students that those who attended all of the sessions would receive gift cards.

## 2011: November 1-6
## (More Planning, More Meetings)

As we moved into the second semester, we had a major faculty meeting on November 2nd to re-emphasize professional responsibilities. Ms. Valdes stressed that every class should have a print rich environment, word walls, common boards, display of current student work, and centers. She told the teachers, "The major rule to classroom discipline is consistency and follow-through. Please make sure that you make parental contact. We do have Saturday detentions where we have a combination of chores and skill-building assignments. Adjust your pacing guides and lesson plans according to the data; your data binder is your classroom bible that drives instruction. Ms. Van Smith has lexiled books for the students to check out from the library, and she can also assist in adding to your classroom libraries. Utilize the cross-curricular reading and writing strategies to increase skills in both. Please make sure that your students work folder is up-to-date with feedback. I have had some delays in getting certain tasks completed because many of you are not reading your e-mails. Please, read your emails. In your electronic grade book, make sure that you have at least two grades recorded with the description of the assignment and a hard copy in a binder. In addition to the two grades, make sure that the grade entries match the lesson plans and the work in the student folder. I know that you have a long paper trail, and Dr. Burnett and I can both testify that what we have to do as teachers and administrators is not indicative of what teachers have to do in non-accountability schools. You need to evaluate your classroom for print rich environment, world walls, common boards, display of current student work, learning centers, classroom management, pacing guides/IFC/lesson plans, explicit instructions/DI/HOT, use of instructional materials/ classroom libraries, and cross content reading/writing. Always make sure that you have on hand your parent contact log, anecdotal log, and emergency sub plans. Dr. Burnett, do you have any announcements?"

I responded, "Thank you. As I always say, I appreciate everything that you do. High school teachers, please do not forget to tell all students that are taking the SAT on Saturday, November 5th and to be prompt with their admission ticket, two number 2 pencils, an acceptable calculator as specified in the instructions, and a photo identification. November 7th-10th is Founders Week. The majority of the activities are after school hours because we do not want to bring any disruption to our classroom environment. On Monday, students should wear their formal wear with a tie for the Monday Assembly. The founding students have prepared a 30-minute assembly. K-2 will go from 8:45 a.m.-9:15 a.m., grades 3-5 will go from 9:30 a.m.-10:00 a.m., 6-8 grades will go from 1:20 p.m.-1:50 p.m. and grades 9-12 will go from 2:10 p.m.-2:40 p.m. The remaining activities are after school. The unveiling of the painting of the late Mr. and Mrs. Allen Lawrence will be on Tuesday at 4:00 p.m.,

Wednesday, there will be a Ribbon Cutting Ceremony at 4:30 p.m., and on Thursday, students can wear their "I am Part of the Vision" t-shirt."

I could say without hesitation, in spite of the occasional gripes and concerns as in any school, they were dedicated and committed to the vision of the school and my parents would have been proud.

## 2011: November 7-13
## (Founders' Week)

I went to pick up my nephew, Khaaliq, at the airport on Saturday, November 5th. He was in graduate school in New York, and had arranged his schedule so he could surprise our students, especially the founding students. He had written and recorded a promotional rap CD for the school in 2005, and we generally played it for PEP rallies, Martin Luther King parade, and other student events. It was not a professionally made CD, but it served its purpose to motivate and inspire students. I was glad to spend some time with my nephew and just catch up on family updates.

On Monday morning, my nephew went with me to school, and I introduced him to the staff. During the interval between visits to classrooms, he completed some college assignments for graduate school in my office. During the elementary assembly, the founding students program included the Pledge of Allegiance, Lawrence Academy Pledge, Moment of Silent Meditation, and the history of Lawrence Academy as told by the students.

The school started in a three-room building with paper on the wall serving as our boards. It ended with the surprise guest, and the elementary students who enjoyed the assembly asked for my nephew's autograph. The response from the middle and high school was different. Both the middle school and high school students enjoyed it, but not as much as the elementary school students. I believe that the older students saw it just as a mere history lesson sprinkled with a little entertainment, and many of them missed the objective of instilling school pride by knowing and understanding the history of the school. This made me realize even more that our greatest impact in making a change in the community would begin with the youngest.

Tuesday, November 8th at 4:00 p.m. the unveiling of the painting of my parents would take place and later it would be mounted in the main office. Carlos Navarro, an old friend and colleague from Design and Architecture Senior High combined an individual photograph that I had of my father with an individual photograph of my mother, to make a powerful painting that defined the essence of dignity, hard work, and perseverance. For the unveiling of the painting, my niece, Kisha Davis, my son, Michael, and I were there for the painting display in the office. I prayed that what my parents represented, and what I was trying to do, would not be in vain. It took every inch of my strength, nerves, and energy to go back at the beginning of each year. My former principal was right in her estimation it would take every fiber in my body to make a margin of progress in this community. Had I regretted my decision to go this route? Regardless of all of the challenges, I honestly could not say that I regretted the decision.

On November 9th, we had a short faculty meeting on the plan for the progress monitoring plan (PMP) before the ribbon cutting ceremony. This gave teachers time to complete the form on line that was due on November 23rd. The ribbon cutting ceremony started at 4:30 p.m. with a ceremonial cutting of the ribbon at the entrance. My husband, children, administrators, and teachers were present as well as the mayor and the owner of the building.

The program started with the invocation, given by my husband, and was followed by "The Star Spangled Banner sung by Reaiah Tyson. Whenever my husband spoke, I always felt his presence as if he was a pastor of a church. He had completed all the coursework for a doctorate in divinity, and even though he always said that he was not "called" to the ministry to preach, it was obvious that he had a ministerial presence. Ms. Althea King gave the welcome and recognized the special guests. As a retired teacher and administrator with over thirty years of experience, she had a way of wooing the audience.

Mayor Wallace gave a very special welcome on behalf of the town of Florida City. Mayor Wallace was instrumental in welcoming Lawrence Academy to Florida City in 2005 when we opened with sixty-three students. Now we had grown to over 400 with the three schools. His daughter had been with us for the previous three years and was the President of the Student Government. Mayor Wallace highlighted the journey of Lawrence Academy and said he enjoyed the Family Nights that we held on the last Friday of each month where he had the opportunity to play chess with my husband. Mayor Wallace had his own Florida City history. Growing up poor in Florida

City, he came out of poverty to become one of the first black mayors in the state of Florida.

The developer of Lawrence Academy followed Mayor Wallace to talk about the Florida City Charter School Project that was in the making for years, and how it was an honor for him to be part of such an illustrious occasion. I had to admit that I felt the developer had both a silver tongue and the gift of gab. Our business dealings with the developer began to open my eyes to the shadiness of doing the business, or perhaps it was just more the reality of doing business. Although the business practices were not illegal, a long list of ethical questions lurked in the back of my mind. I was not surprised that the developer and his entourage exited within minutes after he spoke. Mr. Katz and Ms. Valdes spoke on their connections to Lawrence Academy. Mr. Katz had been with us since 2007-2008 when we had enrolled less than 200 students, and when Ms. Valdes came on board to help in our quest to improve the elementary. She and I had been colleagues at a prominent local high school that received national recognition. Mr. Katz and Ms. Valdes complemented each other, and each of them brought their own unique gifts and talents to help us accomplish our mission, goals, and objectives.

It was refreshing to have Ashley Wallace, President of Student Government and daughter of Mayor Wallace give the history of Lawrence Academy. Ashley shared how, in the past three years, Lawrence Academy's administration and faculty had helped her to improve academically and to become a responsible student. Ashley gained the confidence to tackle academic challenges and aspired to attend college. We had also witnessed how many of our students improved, only to venture to larger campuses. This continued to make it difficult to increase our electives and our ability to offer some sports such as soccer and basketball.

Ms. Scott, our Community Involvement Specialist and President of our Parent Task Force highlighted how she was inspired by the history of Lawrence Academy to become more involved as a parent and later a part-time staff member. She stressed the importance of parental involvement to move Lawrence Academy in the right direction, while soliciting support for parents in the audience, telling them in both English and Spanish that they make ALL THE DIFFERENCE. Ms. Scott, who had migrated to Miami from New York after her father was diagnosed with cancer, was Puerto Rican. She had been a tremendous asset in promoting parental involvement.

I was the last person to speak. I directed my speech to the recently painted portrait of my parents which I called "The Inspiration." "Whether you know it or not, my parents share a history with this community," I said. "Many of our parents are migrants or come from a migrant background. My parents were both sharecroppers from North Carolina, and as many of you, they had dreams and aspirations for their children. The values of thrift and hard work run through the veins of sharecroppers as well as migrant workers. Carlos did an exemplary job depicting years of hard work through the hands of my mother and father. Dressed in their Sunday best was an indication that God was an important aspect of their daily lives. Their eyes show weariness, but strength. They were both proud individuals that taught trustworthiness, respect, responsibility, fairness, and caring by example. It is my hope that Lawrence Academy will uphold the values for which it was founded. I would like to thank my family's unwavering support, the late Mr. Eddie T. Pearson who believed in this vision, the Lawrence Academy Governing Board, and to each one of you so very much for caring enough to come this evening to celebrate our history and our moving to the new facility. At this time, we have student leaders that will take you on a tour of the school, and dinner is provided by Capri Restaurant immediately following the tour."

The ceremony was nice, and as usual the food from Capri Restaurant was excellent. I enjoyed the ceremony and the opportunities for social engagement, but I was mentally and physically exhausted, not from the ceremony, but from the mounting issues of the elementary and our plan to cut spending. The most difficult part was the 30-minute drive home. Melanie rode home with me while Michael rode with his father. She not only was great company, but provided a pleasant way to divert my attention from Lawrence Academy. Melanie was so excited for me to "retell" the history of her grandparents that my exhaustion miraculously disappeared when I began to tell her about random events that occurred when I grew up. She had no idea that she was what the doctor ordered!

I was excited to wear our new blue and gold t-shirt on Thursday, emblazoned with a caution sign on the front with "I am Part of the Vision" and "The Eagles will soar to the Top" on the back. It was nice not only to see all the students but also the staff wearing the t-shirt with pride. The idea was now for the teachers to transform this pride into academic confidence. Gradually, I could feel the culture of Lawrence Academy emerging into what we had envisioned for Florida City. I took the time to take Ileana (Ms. Valdes) to lunch at Cracker Barrel. Ileana insisted on driving, and we left around 11:00 a.m., before Mr.

Katz had to leave at 1:00 p.m. I ordered a vegetable platter and Ileana ordered a Cobb salad. Both of us chatted widely about everything, from the amount of weight that we had gained over the years, to how difficult it is to make a difference in a community that is already at a deficit in so many ways.

"Ileana, so how do you really think things are going?" I asked.

"I think that everything is falling in place. You never truly know how standardized testing will affect your school when it changes every year as it has."

"I know and it goes without saying that in a normal distribution curve, the probability that a student that has traditionally scored low will continue in that percentile. I was reading about a study that shows that in high poverty schools, students are, on average, two years behind academically. Regardless of what labels and statistics say, I just believe that these students can make it, and we will make it. I just want to thank you for taking on such a momentous task," I told her.

"Keitha, you know, I, just like you, left a high performing school because those kids are going to make anyway. These are the kids for whom everything counts, and the teachers count the most," Ileana said.

"And stability," I added. "That is why we applied for the elementary because we already know that the younger the children are, the greater the chance of making a difference. Ileana, there is one thing that I am afraid of and that is time. I am afraid that time is running out. Laws don't take into account that kids just don't have internal clocks that are in line with grade level benchmarks. I know that our kids make progress and studies report that it takes five to ten years for significant change to be made in low performing communities. Laws are not taking that into account. We don't have the money to hire a lobbyist to fight specifically for us in Tallahassee to ensure students have all the supportive services they need," I said.

"We can't save the world. We can only do all we can do and hope for the best. You know I am closely monitoring everything," Ileana replied.

"I know, Ileana, but someone has to take the risk of educating our neediest population. In my estimation, with the increased competition between charters and the school system, there are going to be more kids falling between the cracks, and we truly will become a nation of "the haves and the have-nots." When our education does not effectively take into account reaching our neediest population and the value of education as the greatest equalizer begins to diminish, you can rest assured that a large underclass is going to emerge in our country."

Without hesitation, Ileana replied, "Well, no one can say that we were the ones waiting for other people to do it."

With a smile, I changed the topic. "So, how's your hubby and your girls. I remember when you used to bring your girls to school on teacher's workday."

"Yeah, my husband is going to retire this year and our girls are doing well. Jeanna just got a job as a dietician and Barbara is in graduate school. Keitha, it doesn't take them long to grow up, so you need to make sure that you spend as much time with them as possible."

"In spite of my schedule, I conscientiously make sure that I do. My husband and I already have on our schedule to see '*Happy Feet II*.' It'll be out next week in the theaters."

"It's getting close to twelve o'clock. I guess we need to start heading back. Thank you for lunch, and we have to do this more often. Hopefully, we won't have to talk so much about work,"

"You got it."

By the time we arrived at the school, the high school students were having their lunch. I decided to go to the cafeteria to socialize with the students. They really looked nice in their t-shirts. I had a brief meeting with the Brain Bowl team (Quashay Miller, Jesus Mejia, Diana Cruz, Gracy Monjaras, Gabrielle Scott, Brittany Coll and Kandacy Knights). I gave each one of them the section of the trivia questions and divvied up the required books ranging from the classic, *From Slavery to Freedom* to the contemporary book, *Thriller*. The competition was going to be in January.

Because of winter break, in actuality, that gave us just a little over a month to prepare. These students were committed, and they were excited about competing at FIU.

After meeting with the students, I left about an hour early to spend some time with my nephew. He had spent most of his time completing a couple of papers and relaxing. He enjoyed having the house to himself during the week. He reminded me when he was fourteen years old, and I had assigned him a term paper to complete during the summer. To his dismay, I had given a "C". We both looked back at it with humor.

The entire family took Khaaliq to the airport on Saturday evening. Michael enjoyed having someone to play basketball with after school. Khaaliq gave us a break when he served as a babysitter. On Friday night, Michael and I were able to enjoy an evening out, something that we both needed. After everyone got their last hug, we watched until he disappeared into the terminal.

## 2011: November 14-20
## (More Testing…More Meetings)

We administered mid-year teacher assessment for third-graders on November 15th and 16th to identify potential failures on the 2011-2012 FCAT 2.0. Only a small percentage was potential failures based on the interim assessments. Those students would have an opportunity to pass based on their performance on a portfolio.

A Leadership Meeting was held on November 15th to continue the discussion on the progress of the elementary school and to also discuss the large percentage of parent meetings conducted by Ms. Valdes based on a significant number of students that were not attending tutoring sessions, but were required to attend because they failed to make adequate progress. The consistency paid off, and the majority of the students were in tutoring. A special parent night had been planned for March 2012 to give parents last minute tips to help their child prepare for the FCAT. An FCAT Pep Rally was also scheduled on April 13th, four to six weeks leading up to the FCAT for the elementary, middle and high school. A professional development workshop for all students on test taking tips was also scheduled.

The coaches had identified material with the highest content focus for the reading and math winter packets. Teachers would review the winter packets in class during the week they returned. In addition, 5th grade would be given a science packet. There would also be a reading plus contest during the winter break.

It was agreed that the baseline would be repeated February 29, 2012, and the data would be reviewed with the child. The spring packets would be targeted to reach the needs of each student. After spring break, a benchmark would be covered each day until the FCAT. The second series of interventions for reading would start after the winter interim. Everyone was updated on fire safety and discipline. A major issue that was raised was the procedure for response to intervention. It began to appear that Ms. Grambling was not clear on most of the questions that were posed to her by CSO, which proved problematic because neither my area nor Ms. Valdes' was special education. Nevertheless, it was evident that she was not the expert we assumed she was based on her interview and her resume.

# 2011: November 21-27
# (The Eagle's Nest, A Labor of Love in the Midst of Directives)

A major faculty meeting was held November 22nd. At the faculty meetings, teachers were informed that data chats would be scheduled for Wednesday, November 23rd. The faculty was reminded of the charter school compliance review scheduled for December 13$^{th}$, and given a to-do-list that they had seen countless times before. After the general meeting, the faculty divided into two groups, elementary and secondary.

Ms. Valdes presided over the elementary, while Dr. Middlebrooks presided over the secondary. In the elementary meeting, Ms. Valdes and the elementary teachers continued to discuss the charter school compliance review, differentiated accountability, data chats after each assessment, interventions for grades 3-5, ELL, K-2 and non-ELL students. Teachers were given a schedule for the individual teacher meeting that would be held on November 29$^{th}$. The other issues discussed with the secondary teachers, beyond the intervention schedule in reading, math, and science, were the dismissing of students early from class and limiting bathroom passes. At the conclusion of the meeting, teachers were given a schedule for individual meetings with Mr. Katz on December 1$^{st}$. Ms. Valdes had made two homemade cakes for the teachers. It was that personal touch that always soothed the sting of the seriousness of the school's plight.

Sharon Van Smith, our librarian was excited to announce that Miami-Dade County Public Library System had scores of books that they were disposing of, and she was more than happy to begin picking them up. Our library ballooned from 7,000 volumes to nearly 13,000. She affectionately called the library our "Eagle's Nest." After her retirement from Miami-Dade Public Schools, I was happy she agreed to come aboard and help us build a library. It was quaint and aesthetically deco-rated. She recruited one of her former students to volunteer to organize the library and to develop a library webpage that would be linked to our major homepage. I did not know until a year later that Sharon had paid her student a stipend to get our library running smoothly. It was these types of things that made Lawrence Academy special.

Right before Thanksgiving break, my husband and I had decided to withdraw Michael from his home school. He was not adjusting well in traditional public school, and I began to second guess our decision to withdraw him from Lawrence Academy due to my long days after school. The best decision at this point was to home school him. Re-enrolling him at Lawrence Academy was not fair to the teachers, particularly under the current circumstances. I decided to get the lesson plans and assignments from my teachers to use as a guideline. My office had two desks and was well suited to accommodate my new assistant. He was thrilled that he would be returning to Lawrence Academy.

This reminded me of a similar situation. I had advised one of my employees to withdraw her daughter from public school and to place her in home school. Her daughter was two grades behind as a result of the mandatory retention of students that do not perform at a certain level at grade three. She had shown dramatic improvement over the past two years, but there was no opportunity to place her in the correct grade in the public school setting. After home school for one year, her work was assessed by two certified teachers, and she took the FCAT for her correct grade. She performed adequately on the teacher assessments and the FCAT. At the end of the year, she was eligible to be placed in her correct grade. The following year, Lawrence Academy enrolled her in her correct grade level. My son's own academic struggles made me ultra-sensitive to all students that are struggling academically and need a remedy that will give them confidence in their own ability.

The two-day Thanksgiving break was a relief from the everyday demands of school. The holiday tradition with turkey and all the trimmings was a must in our household. It gave us a chance to entertain some of our family members and friends. We had needed to wind down and relax so that all of us would be renewed for Monday morning.

## 2011: November 28-30
## (Efforts to Build a Community Coalition)

The major agenda driving this week was the commencing of FAIR testing, which would continue until February 2nd. After a four-day break, it was not surprising to find students and teachers in a somber mood. The absentee rate was above the normal among the students. As I quickly did some classroom walk-throughs, I noticed that many teachers had incorporated some hands-on activities as a way to get the students back on task. Michael enjoyed being back at Lawrence Academy, even though he was with me for most of the day. We had a routine. He would do his silent reading in the morning, followed by selected math problems. In the afternoons, he would work on science and computer-based programs.

I was glad Michael could attend the afterschool program sponsored by The Children's Trust and WeCare. I did not feel as guilty if I had to stay after school for an extended period of time. With the new facility, we had begun to attract some more community-based programs, as I had envisioned for Lawrence

Academy. It was a very difficult project in the midst of ongoing retrenchment of social spending. We had at least ten different organizations that were providing in-kind services to Lawrence Academy; however, we were still unable to secure any major grants, sponsors, or donors. I soon learned the strides made with Harlem Kids' Zone project were unprecedented and difficult to replicate. While achievement was not where it should be for the elementary, it was undeniable that Lawrence Academy was an asset to the children of Florida City. My feeling of urgency and my need to help the community was something that gave me the drive to "make it happen."

Ms. Valdes' Phase 1 of tutorials scheduled afterschool and on Saturdays continued throughout the month of November, as did the Boy Scouts on Tuesdays/Saturdays and the Fatherhood Program on Wednesdays. The month ended with an ice cream party for all honor roll students in elementary, middle and high school.

## 2011: December 1-4
## (Seeking Peace in the Eye of the Storm)

The festive month of December began with a Leadership Team meeting scheduled at 10:30 a.m. with updates on the elementary and secondary schools, RTI, and the upcoming CSO Curriculum and Compliance Review on December 13th. Opening the month with a major meeting was an indication of the work that still needed to be done. The needs of the majority of our student population seemed exhaustive. In the back of my mind lurked the recurring thoughts of what-ifs, particularly if our charter focused on a needy population of students. I knew the work that had been done would yield tenfold in results. On every occasion, the intrinsic part of me would confirm there was a purpose for this, no matter what the outcome. There were indeed some hard-core issues and policies in education that still had not been addressed effectively, particularly when it came to serving the disadvantaged and underserved populations. I was inspired to begin journaling weekly by a segment on Oprah in which she expressed the benefits of journaling, I began journaling and it allowed me to, not only acknowledge what was occurring, but to process what was occurring. Probably more so than ever before, I began to realize that "my world" could easily crumble like a stack of cards; however, there were two stabilizing factors in my life, my faith and my family. I decided to take a break. On Friday, December 1st, I made the decision that my daughter and I would skip school and have a mother/daughter weekend. We headed to Orlando to see Joel Osteen and Disney!!

## 2011: December 5-11
## (From Idealism to Realism)

After the Joel Osteen weekend with my daughter, Monday, December 5th, I felt re-energized and ready to conquer the world. During the walkthrough with the elementary, I asked the students to tell me the meaning of the pine cone that I had given their teachers. In unison, they would echo, "wisdom and strength!" I had made it a tradition to give the elementary teachers a pine cone from my home town of Rocky Mount, North Carolina to place in their room as a symbol of confidence. I still believed in the heart of my dissertation entitled, "An Economic Evaluation of Alternative High School Settings:

The Significance of Assessing Cost-Effectiveness of Magnet Schools vs. Traditional Schools."

Even though the focus of my dissertation was geared toward a cost-effectiveness model, it attempted to explore and unearth the impact of Bandura's elusive term of "self-efficacy" on academic achievement which can have an impact on cost. Self-efficacy is defined as an individual's confidence and capability to organize and implement a specific set of actions to successfully perform a given task.

The findings of the Coleman Report of 1968 revealed that a student's background was the primary determinant of academic achievement. The dissertation claims that if this is the case, then to my thinking attributing students' academic achievement to the curriculum of magnet schools is premature. This is not to imply that a school's academic achievement is insignificant, but its relationship to academic achievement may account for only a partial change in academic achievement. Thus, Bandura's self-efficacy could be one of the keys to unraveling underachievement among students at risk. Even though Bandura's theory of self-efficacy is more profound than a "wisdom and strength" recitation, it was a beginning for a group of students that needed some positive reinforcement.

Ms. Scott, the community involvement specialist, briefed me on the Parent Task Force meeting that was held on December 3rd. The highlight of the meeting was fundraising that could reduce the cost of senior activities, and setting up a payment plan that would alleviate the overwhelming cost of the senior year.

After school, Ms. Valdes and I reviewed the items for the board meeting, faculty meeting, and the holiday luncheon scheduled on early release. Phase 1 of the Saturday Academy, the after-school tutoring, as well as the intervention groups, were fully operational. The Holiday Drop-off was scheduled for four days during the winter break: December 20th, 21st, 27th, and 28th. The purpose of the holiday drop-off was to provide support for students to complete their winter packets. Initially, I had expressed to Ms. Valdes the importance of informing teachers about the three furlough days before the holidays. Ms. King and I had decided originally to have a conference with each teacher on December 6th, but changed it to January 5th since there was flexibility among the teachers regarding what days to select. Additionally, we did not want to spoil the spirit of the holiday season. The energy that I had in the morning could easily have been measured on a Richter scale, but now it had been reduced so low it would be undetectable.

On December 6th, there were two major items on my agenda: meeting with the owner and a faculty meeting after school. For all major meetings, Ms. King was present. She arrived around 8:30 a.m. with her coffee in one hand and her Lawrence Academy notebook in another. As chairperson, she made sure she kept a detailed record of what occurred in each meeting. Ms. King understood the values upon which Lawrence Academy was founded, that of "free and appropriate" education, equity, character education, and the desire that every child has the opportunity to pursue their education beyond high school. It was these values that led us to make many of the decisions that would be detrimental to us in the long run.

Ms. King said, "Keitha, you are looking tired."

"Just so much on my mind and I wonder if is it all worth it," I told her. "Between the elementary, the shrinking budget, the building, the district, and the state, I just want to give up. When does it end or at least let up?"

"Just keep your chin up. You' are doing a great job. There are extenuating that circumstances that have made it difficult for us. I just see conflicting values between your vision and the laws and guidelines that are placed at the district and state level," Ms. King said.

I quickly said, "My husband and I had so many dreams for this community, and that may be the problem. You can't dream for others."

"Keitha, it's not that you're dreaming for them. You are providing an opportunity that otherwise would not be available to this population. Beyond the philosophical discussion, we have some real issues to deal with now. The developer/owner is going to be here in an hour. What are we requesting?" replied Ms. King.

"We need a plan that will keep his interest, and that is how he will benefit. After the fact, we have literally been screwed in some regards, but we have also benefitted with a facility that is one of the most elegant buildings in Florida City, with amenities that will help with recruitment and our reaccreditation in 2013. In order to move forward, we need to make sure he knows we are committed to this facility, and the expansion to a second building for the elementary and the middle and high school addition," I replied.

PART I (WISDOM AND STRENGTH)

Ms. King asked, "What is the population enrollment cap for each school according to your charter?"

"Four to five hundred, I am pretty sure," I replied.

"Getting our grade up for the elementary will automatically give us some positive publicity for recruitment purposes. What kind of concessions are we asking for now?" Ms. King asked.

"We need to look at trying to reduce the lease payment, pure and simple."

"We're meeting with the teachers on January 5th. Do you have a copy of the furlough proposal?" Ms. King asked.

"I have the copy of the reduction sheet here. Teachers have to take four furlough days, and they can select what four days they want. They are scheduled from January to June. We really have taken into consideration the best means of reducing the budget without placing a major strain on the majority of the employees."

"How do you save money?" Ms. King asked. "You will need substitutes to cover the teachers."

"No, they are scheduled on planning days or holidays," I replied. I spoke into the phone. "Thanks. Tell him to come up."

"Ms. King, he's here. He's coming up."

"I see that you are taking a 20 percent cut and the art teacher will become part-time, among other things," replied Ms. King.

In less than five minutes, the developer/owner was walking through the door. He was more pleasant than usual, perhaps because the holiday season was drawing near.

During the 45-minute meeting, we went back and forth on reducing the lease. He finally stated that he would wait and see toward the end of the year when we had a better idea about the elementary school. The answer was essentially not a "yes" or "no."

After the meeting, Ms. King and I escorted him to his car since we were going to lunch. We had lunch at Cracker Barrel and headed back to the school by 12:30 p.m. so that Ms. King could work with the fourth graders.

The faculty meeting was scheduled in room 302 after school, and I started the meeting by thanking the faculty and staff for everything they do, seen and unseen. I did not stay for the remainder of the meeting. Ms. Valdes conducted the meeting, highlighting the Charter School Office Compliance Visit scheduled for December 13th.

Before going home, I picked up Michael from the after-school program and we made a stop at my favorite little spot, Starbucks. I had frequented it so much that everyone knew my favorite drink, which was a grande cappuccino with four raw sugars topped with whipped cream. Michael had an organic milk with a muffin. Michael went to our favorite space in the corner with his goodies and his *Diary of a Wimpy Kid*. Right next to him, I just relaxed on the couch with one of Dr. Stanley's books, *How to Handle Adversity*. Dr. Stanley's books were always inspirational, with practical advice based on biblical teachings. Dr. Stanley's teachings had been an influential part of my life for nearly two decades. While I sought to make sense of life, Michael just enjoyed being with mommy.

December 8th was early release and the school's holiday luncheon. Teachers and staff had a full spread of holiday meats, vegetables, salads, starches, bread, and dessert. With the holiday music and the gift exchange, the spirit of the holiday season was all around us. As always, I began the luncheon by thanking the teachers and staff for all they do. Mr. Katz and Ms. Valdes presented each teacher with a Starbucks gift card as an expression of our appreciation. With an extended lunch, everyone enjoyed the celebration with food and fellowship.

Workshops were scheduled the last hour of the day. Dr. Middlebrooks was the facilitator for the high school reading strategies; Ms. Blandon, high school math; Dr. Olivia, K-2 common core; Ms. Baptiste, mathematics IFCs; and Ms. Lara, reading/writing.

I had a Governing Board meeting that night at 6:00 p.m. Michael and I picked up Melanie after school at around 3:00 p.m. Before heading home, we stopped by Publix to pick up several items for dinner before I went back to school for the board meeting. It was important for me that my kids had a healthy meal in spite of my busy schedule. When Michael, Sr. arrived home around 5:30 p.m., I had dinner prepared, and my meeting materials packed to return to Lawrence Academy for the meeting. The meeting was attended by Lula Pearson, Christina Garcia, Melvin Dennis, Ken Cooper, Althea King and a potential member, Ted Greer.

The meeting was called to order at 6:10 p.m. I reviewed the benchmarks from the Charter School's visit on compliance, scheduled for December 13th and the required informational meeting on the renewal process for the elementary. Ms. King stated that new attorneys were being interviewed after the termination of our present attorney.

A meeting with the developer resulted in some possible concessions on the monthly rent. Unexpected expenditures as a result of the move had brought about concerns regarding the budget. The board approved the proposed budget reduction plan.

Ms. Valdes presented a report on the status of the elementary. She showed the progress that had been made in the bi-weekly assessments and the mid-year test. The teachers were diligently working and the data conclusively showed that progress was being made. Saturday enrollment had increased. There would be another interim test on January 10th. There had been a grant received for $5,000 for ESOL tutoring for grades K-2. A reminder was given to parents that the FCAT would be administered April 16th-27th.

There was a plan to strengthen the Legal and Public Affairs Academy for the following year by providing on the job training. Many students did not have transportation, but potential positions had been identified at City Hall, COFFO, Department of Children and Families, First Assembly, and the Police Department. The board approved the participation of Lawrence Academy in the Recapturing the Vision program for 2012. It was a program for high school students that focused on teen issues and family mentoring. The meeting was adjourned at 7:52 p.m.

On Friday, December 9th, the high school students had planned a trip to Santa's Enchanted Forest. I was looking forward to being one of the chaperones. The great thing about Lawrence Academy was that we never had a problem enlisting teachers to chaperone trips outside the school day. They all knew the importance of our students having positive and safe activities outside of school time. The bus was scheduled to leave at 5:00 p.m. which gave students a chance to go home to freshen up and return by that deadline. My entire family was recruited to go. Michael and I left slightly earlier to pick up Melanie, and to go home to freshen up as well. We had to be back to the school by 4:30 p.m. to meet the early arrivals.

Michael Sr. was going to meet us at Santa's after work. The other chaperones were there by the time I arrived. They had organized the trip, requiring everyone to be in a group of at least three, but not more than five. There was a leader for each group. The leaders were required to call the designated chaperone on the hour. It was decided that everyone would meet at the large Christmas treat at the evening halfway mark, which was 9:00 p.m. for a checkpoint. This had always worked well.

It was a great feeling to see the kids enjoying themselves. All the cares of their reality appeared to be instantaneously washed away. It also gave my family a chance to have some down time as well, even though I kept a watchful eye on our students as we perused throughout Santa's, getting a moment here and there to interact with them. The most memorable was the Crazy Mouse ride. The ride looked harmless, but once it started, it was more than I had bargained for. Through our facial expressions, the photos taken at strategic points on the ride captured all the emotions that surfaced. We purchased the photo, and I could not believe the sense of fear that was on my husband's face! The students were able to pull me back on the ride and I acquiesced. We later took a family picture as Santa's reindeer, and could not resist the temptation to indulge in the carnival goodies.

As it was approaching 11:30 p.m., it was time to head to the bus, and everyone, for the most part, was in place by 11:45 p.m. My kids went home with my husband, and I rode back to the school with the students and chaperones on the bus. In spite of the less than desirable 45-minute haul back to the school, the bus that had once been lively on the way to Santa's was now very quiet with more sleeping students than awake. Whenever I gazed over my shoulders to check on the students, it gave me a sense of pleasure and pride because they were indeed "my children." We arrived back to the school around 12:30 a.m., and the last student pick-up was around 1:00 a.m. Then, I was on my way home, the conclusion of another day.

Phase I of Saturday tutoring was still in progress. After a full week topped with a late-night fieldtrip, I had informed Ms. Valdes that I would not be there. We talked later that day and she was pleased with the attendance. My husband went to the school during the early afternoon for the Boy Scouts meeting; the regular faithful twelve to fifteen boys attended. I could see the positive impact on the students' behavior, and their sense of civic duty. Ms. Scott coordinated the high school senior car wash in front of the school to help in their efforts to raise money to reduce the overall cost of their graduation expenses. The never-ending calendar of tutorials, meetings, and activities was a precursor of what was to come in the upcoming months.

Sunday was a special day for us. After a splendid church service on Sunday, Michael wanted to spend his birthday at Chuck E. Cheese. We allowed him to invite one of his good friends from church, and we spent the evening stuffing our face with wings, and pizza, and competing to see who could collect the most tickets. It was amusing to see adults as well as kids spend twenty or thirty dollars just to win the grand prize of a small stuffed animal.

## 2011: December 12-18
## (In spite of….Celebrating the Holiday Season)

It was clear the holiday season was in the air when you walked into Lawrence Academy. The Christmas tree in the office, and all the trimmings throughout the school, placed everyone in the holiday spirit. You could even feel the spirit of the holiday season by the expression in everyone's smile, their walk and general demeanor. Students were buzzing about Secret Santa, Polar Express, and scores of other holiday festivities. I wondered what the world would be like if every day could capture the essence of the holiday seasons. The visit from the district scheduled for the 13th could not dampen the infectious spirit of the holiday. Ms. Valdes and Mr. Katz had prepared the documents needed for the compliance visit, and the teachers were well-prepared. They had plenty of dress-rehearsals.

Later that day, Ms. Hawkins had students distribute the first Lawrence Academy Eagle News with the headline story, "Volunteer This Christmas" by Nick Evelyn and the quote of the month, "Be more concerned with your character than your reputation. Your character is what you really are, while your reputation is merely what others think you are.—John Wooden."

The seniors began to hold bake sales after school on a more consistent basis, and their primary customers were the elementary students. The senior bake sale became a favorite "stop over" before going to tutoring.

I ended the day helping Ms. Valdes with a few minor details in preparing for the compliance visit. As usual, we stayed a little longer since most teachers wanted to make sure everything was in place for the next day.

The compliance visit for the middle and high school went swiftly as we had expected; however, there was always something else that needed to be done for the elementary. There were still issues with the paper trail for the SPED population, and I could not understand why everything could not be resolved. Neither Ms. Valdes nor I had the expertise to follow through on correcting the problems. We only had about thirty SPED students total. We had done better as far as the paper trail was concerned, using a part-time SPED specialist that we had used the year before. One thing I knew for sure: I was going to present to the board a request to have our SPED teacher's contract terminated immediately after the holiday. There was no excuse for someone with a masters and presently working on a doctorate with seven years of SPED experience in Miami-Dade County Schools to not be able to follow through on what was required. We had hired a full-time SPED specialist to provide additional support to our SPED and ELL students, and it was not occurring, at least not based on the documentation.

On December 15th, Ms. Valdes and I went to the required contract meeting that was held at Downtown Charter. Our new attorney, Albert Dotson, made me realize the difficulty that we were confronted with by having to go up for renewal at a time when all of our energy needed to go toward raising our school grade. According to our attorney, the board should not have presented any contract changes at the informal meet we had on June 16th, in light of the fact that our former attorney was not present. They took advantage of our Governing Board Chair being present. Our once ten-year contract was reduced to four years. At the time, I felt that something could have been negotiated at that time based on previous increases in academic achievement of the middle and high school, and the legislation in Tallahassee to increase the number of years a school has to improve its grade.

The meeting was facilitated by Ms. Coleman and scores of handouts and checklists were distributed. The renewal process was not an easy undertaking, but Ms. Valdes and I were confident that we could handle the application process. We felt the rigor of the politics was now out of our league. Nevertheless, we did feel better about our new attorney, who appeared to be more experienced and savvy than the former. He consulted with Ms. Valdes and me on a regular basis.

The renewal meeting lasted only about an hour, and we left immediately afterwards to Florida City. We arrived at Lawrence Academy at the end of the elementary lunch. I used the time to visit the middle and high school classes. They were busy decorating their doors for the judging scheduled later that day. I was amazed to see the competitive spirit among the various classroom teams in their efforts to secure a first prize for a pizza party. At the end of the day, Ms. Barrios' homeroom emerged as the victor.

On Friday, the elementary school students came dressed in their pajamas, ready for their Polar Express event with hot chocolate and movies. Ms. Valdes made sure that all of them were given a reminder letter about the required "Holiday Drop-off" scheduled for December 20th, December 21st, December 27th and December 28th from 9:00 a.m.-1:00 p.m. I volunteered for the 20th and 21st. Since we knew students had little support at home to get the packets completed during the break, the major goal was to have the students complete and review the winter packets which included the benchmarks of students who had the most problems. The number of students had thinned out by the end of the day, coupled with the high absenteeism and parents picking their children up early to get a jumpstart on the holiday celebrations. We did not mind as long as they remembered the dates for the Holiday Drop-off.

The final Saturday for the Phase 1 was December 17th. The attendance was lower than usual, but that was expected. Ms. Valdes used Saturday morning to call the parents personally to remind them about the importance of the Holiday Drop-off, while I checked my emails and drafted a letter to the board recommending the termination of our SPED specialist.

## 2011: December 19-25 (One More Tutorial Session Just Before the Holidays)

Most teachers opted out on December 19th, a teacher's planning day, to extend their winter break. I used the day to organize and file papers. It is amazing how quickly papers accumulate in such a short amount of time, even in the age of technology.

I could only imagine what my office would look like next semester when, as a result of budget reductions, I'd start teaching two critical thinking classes, one for middle and one for high school.

When I arrived on Tuesday to supervise the Holiday Drop-off, there were several students already standing at the door. Ms. Lara had extra packets in case they had been forgotten or misplaced. After the first session, Ms. Lara saw that only two days were needed, so we cancelled the two days after Christmas. December 27th and 28th. On Wednesday, Mr. Cruz came in to help students complete and review the math portion of their packets. After 1:00 p.m. on December 21st when the last parent picked up his/her child, I was officially on Christmas break. I had made a vow to myself that I would not do anything related to Lawrence Academy until January 3rd.

We had decorated our tree the day after Thanksgiving. I purchased additional lights and decorations for the outside. Michael made sure the lights were up the week following Thanksgiving, giving us time to enjoy the added dimension of the joyous season. As part of our Christmas tradition, I allowed Melanie to invite a couple of her friends over to bake cakes and cookies. I was not surprised that her friends had not used dry and liquid measuring utensils in the kitchen. A quick practical math class was always part of the fun. Little Michael would always pitch in more in the interest of eating the cookies than baking them. At the end, her friends were proud to take their baked goods home. It was an exhausting activity that would send Melanie and Michael to bed early enough for Mommy and Daddy to play Santa. We would start a couple of days before Christmas just in case things did not go as planned. Of course, Melanie no longer believed in Santa, but she continued the charade to make it more exciting for Michael, and the gifts from Santa under the tree were definitely an incentive. She encouraged Michael to place a couple of cookies and a glass of milk on the coffee table. Michael and I would nibble off the cookies and drink a couple of sips from the glass of milk for authenticity. The cherubic expression on cherubic Michael's face when he saw the nibbled cookies and the vanished milk was enough to soften the heart of a villain.

This year, the major gift for the kids was bikes. Michael and I had our old bikes. After our morning of thanks and a hearty breakfast, Michael stacked the bikes on the car rack and we headed to the park. I think everyone else in our neighborhood had the same idea. Even though Michael's bike had training wheels, he tried his best to challenge Melanie in a race to no avail. After a couple of hours in the park riding the bikes and tossing a baseball, we had reached our limit of outdoor activity. Besides, we had planned to leave the following day to Rocky Mount, North Carolina to visit my family. Everyone was accustomed to the routine and was packed by nightfall.

## 2011: December 26-31 (A Cure for the Blues)

We were on 95 north by 8:00 a.m. We stopped only for gas and bathroom stops until we arrived in Savannah, where we took a break. We did a little bit of shopping at the outlet malls, and had dinner at Denny's. The temperature had dropped even more by the time we left Savannah, and the kids were asleep by the time we hit the county line. It was almost midnight when we arrived in Rocky Mount. We only took a couple of bags out of the car since it was so late, and Mary, my oldest sister, was at the door to greet us. It felt so good to be home on Main Street!!

Michael and the kids were tired and went straight to bed, but I was re-energized enough to catch up on the family gossip with my sisters until the wee hours of the morning. I was still the first one to get up, and I prepared the expected breakfast of bacon, eggs, grits, and waffles. Everyone trickled in one by one, and my brother, Joseph, who lived only several blocks away, joined us for breakfast.

With Mary, Shirley and my family in the family house, we decided to stay with my brother for the remainder of the visit. We had planned periodic outings and visits for the following three days to visit with family and friends. The kids had a great time with their cousins, and they enjoyed the camaraderie. In the midst of a busy schedule in connecting with family, I took the time to visit the site of our old church in Tarboro that was destroyed by Hurricane Floyd. The pine tree next to the tracks was able to withstand the devastation. It was somewhat of a pilgrimage for me that gave me solace. On my knees, this had become my place to talk to God, and I could feel his presence. From family, marriage, and my inner most thoughts, He was my refuge; however, I could never get a grip and a spirit of contentment with issues concerning Lawrence Academy. There was silence. At the base of my knee was a pine cone. I could hear the elementary kids echo "wisdom and strength," in unison after I prompted them by asking them what did the pine cone represent. I had given the elementary teachers a pine cone from this very tree for their classroom. Deep in my spirit, I knew the issues related to Lawrence Academy, and education in general, were as complex as the design of the pine cone, and the current legislation was not comprehensive enough to address them. Countless times, it crossed my mind from the inception of Lawrence Academy that I should have done what many charters had been accused of doing, resorting to "creaming" and data manipulation, but I held true to the concept that our charter had an open door policy and the premise that every child can learn.

As the wind whistled through the trees, coupled with the chill in the air, I felt at peace and understood and accepted that the end of Lawrence Academy could easily be imminent. I felt, however, I would be given the strength to endure whatever the outcome would be. Failure in the eyes of the world did not equate to failure in the spiritual realm. I left my thoughts on that church ground that day as I traveled the fifteen miles back to Rocky Mount. I took a detour to visit the gravesite of my mom and dad, the inspiration for Lawrence Academy. It became clear to me even though the brick-and-mortal Lawrence Academy could cease to exist, what was inside of me could never end, not even in death.

On Friday, our family met at the Hibachi Grill for lunch. With nearly twenty people in our group, it felt like a small family reunion. The food was great, but the closeness and the energy I felt with my family created a sustaining force of purpose and direction. It was hard to believe that it had been forty-five years since our family left the farm to move to the city, and now we had scattered and settled along the east coast with families of our own. I had always said if it hadn't been for my husband, I would have moved closer to home. Even now, it was difficult when the time came to return to Miami. Since family was important to me, the concept of family was one of the major tenets of Lawrence Academy.

Our last major family gathering before we returned to Miami was to our family's home church, Hart's Chapel Baptist Church. This was a great way to start out the New Year. The new edifice was located in a suburban section of Rocky Mount which had taken the place of the original church in Tarboro. The most appealing aspect of our church is the simplicity and genuineness of worship since the family is one of the major tenets of our worship that brought support and solidarity. I also incorporated this concept of family in the development of Lawrence Academy. After a Spirit-filled sermon, and a chance to reconnect with family and friends, I always left feeling more uplifted, focused and re-energized since our mom had passed away. Sunday was not Sunday without the traditional Sunday dinner spread that was prepared by my oldest sister. Shirley, Deloris and I always assisted, but she took the lead. The driver, Michael, took a nap after dinner because we were scheduled to leave at 6:00 p.m. After a good game of spades, a monopoly game, television, and catching up on the latest gossip of Rocky Mount, time just slipped away. It was time for us to gather our belongings and head back to Miami. It was always an emotional departure with hugs, tearful eyes, and sad goodbyes. Our car was always solemn for the first hour or so of the ride home to Miami.

# PART II
## (Countdown to FCAT)

# 2012: January 2-8
## (Ready, Set, Go…Phase II Tutorials)

With just a few stops, we were back in Miami by 8:00 a.m. Monday morning. We had ample time to relax and mentally prepare for the school and work routine on the next day, but nevertheless, as in most households throughout Miami-Dade County with school age children, it was a struggle.

Phase II of the tutorials were operational on Tuesday. The after school Reading Plus labs were scheduled for Tuesday and Thursday. The science and writing camps were scheduled on Saturday, and the reading and math enrichment commenced the first week of February. We had our Leadership team meeting promptly at 10:00 a.m. Briefly, after everyone greeted each other with a Happy New Year, Ms. King called the meeting to order. The items on the agenda were the review of the status of the elementary, the crunch schedule for the middle and high school, preparation of state visit on February 13th, budget planning/recruitment, and a rescheduled meeting with teachers. Ms. Valdes reviewed the data, which indicated the fourth graders were not proficient in writing. The majority of the students were at level 1 and 2. Additionally, the fourth graders had the lowest percentage of students reading at proficiency. Ms. King, whose certification was in English, had tutored the lowest five students since October, and we had made sure that Ms. Lara, our reading coach, spent at least 50 percent of her time with this group. The FCAT Writing was scheduled for February 28th - March 1st. The winter interims were scheduled during January 9th - January 20th. Mr. Katz reviewed the computer schedule that he had set up for middle and high school students to spend at least three days in the computer lab a week, which started in October. We discussed in detail the issues with recruitment for the following year. We had already sent out postcards to potential students, but we knew our success with recruitment hinged on the success of the elementary. The data, supporting documents for the issues raised in the first state visit were corrected, and, as far as the guidelines and procedures, we were on auto-pilot with the exception of special education. Ms. King and I had scheduled a meeting with each teacher for Wednesday after lunch.

The teachers had the schedule, and one-by-one Ms. King and I told them what would be occurring effective immediately. But the two of us had decided that it would be better to present it after the holidays, since there was flexibility in the days that would be cut. We reviewed items on the budget that could not be compromised, such as costs related to moving, and the required change of most of the elementary textbooks. The textbooks took us by surprise, because most of the elementary books were less than two years old, and the material covered in the books was not drastically different.

After the overview, we told each teacher/staff member about the reductions that needed to be made. Before introducing how the proposed cuts would affect them, Ms. King prefaced it with the fact that the greatest reduction was from the top, which was me with an 18 percent reduction in pay. With that being said, the teachers welcomed the four-day furlough days that could be taken at their convenience on the specified days. Before we reached the middle of the list, the news had already spread to everyone, which made each one much easier to complete. It took the entire afternoon, with only a few minutes to spare before the end of school. Ms. King was totally exhausted after spending the entire day at Lawrence Academy. I thanked her as usual and reminded her about the board meeting on Thursday.

I left with Michael directly after school so that I could return for the governing board meeting, but before we left, Michael wanted something from the senior bake sale. With Michael, it was by default that I supported all of the sales. I didn't mind, because I was so proud of the initiative that Becky took to organize fundraisers to reduce the costs of graduation expenses for her class. I quickly prepared dinner as Melanie and Michael began their homework. I was running late, because Michael Sr. was running late from work. The meeting was called to order at 6:18 p.m. by Ms. King. The minutes were read and approved. I informed the board that the accountant's report would be ready at the end of the month and a loan request had been placed at three different banks. All board members would keep abreast of requests. The intercom system was scheduled to be completed by the following week. We needed 200 students for the following year to be at an optimal level of students to costs. Also, we needed to increase our enrollment by thirty students by the end of January.

Ms. King then stated that an employee was at the meeting to appeal for reinstatement. She was terminated by Dr. Burnett as a result of showing an "R" rated movie. The movie had no academic content, and, additionally, she did not follow procedures by getting approval to show movies. After hearing her appeal to reinstate based on her promise that she would not do it again, the governing board unanimously voted to reject her appeal since it had been documented that she'd been given a warning about a similar situation earlier in the year, but she was given the option to resign from her position.

The Governing Board agreed on designing an aggressive plan for grant-writing. Our present attorney was terminated and would be able to receive his final payment upon the receipt of Lawrence Academy's files. The next meeting would be held on March 8th at 6:00 p.m. The meeting was adjourned at 7:30 p.m. Having the meeting at 6:00 p.m. was much better for me than 7:00 p.m., I was able to make my usual stop at Starbucks for my perfect grande cappuccino with a moment to relax and reflect.

Saturday, January 8th was busier than usual. After the writing and science workshops, Michael and several boy and cub scouts' parents were preparing to march in the Martin Luther King Parade. I saw Ms. Scott, our community liaison, who reminded me that the voting of the king and queen, representing each school for the Martin Luther King Parade, was on Monday. At the same time, we had detentions, which I monitored. Students cleaned the desks, walls, and picked up trash on the campus. For our student population, it appeared that cleaning up was not a deterring factor. In fact, many of them enjoyed cleaning. I assumed that it was probably a part of their home responsibility, and they would be expected to do an excellent job. I have to admit, they did just that. The building was not cleared until about 4:00 p.m. Michael stayed to lock up the building, while my kids and I went to get groceries. This was one of our busier Saturdays.

There was no doubt that everyone was tired on Sunday morning, but we made the effort to have our usual large Sunday breakfast before church. We were never disappointed when we made the decision to go to church.

This was one of those Sunday evenings, when Michael and I had a long discussion about our hopes, fears and challenges ahead. We had considered the possibility that moving was probably the worst decision in the midst of this grade crisis, but at the same time, there were legitimate concerns raised by the board with issues related to overall safety of the previous building. We had conquered grade issues in the past, and there was no reason it could not be duplicated, but there were real concerns emerging. The standards had changed during the previous two years, and the cut scores for each level were being raised, but we also had one-hundred percent of our teachers highly qualified, and we had more resources, more support for our leadership, a better environment for learning, and an increased level of workshops and tutorials for the students. There was no doubt that the level of commitment was exceptional, but in the back of my mind, study after study showed schools with similar student populations could take up to 5-7 years to show a significant improvement and we were just on the third year.

## 2012: January 9-15 (Too Many Battles)

On Monday, January 9th, the students voted during homeroom for queen and king for the Martin Luther King's Parade. Winter interims were scheduled from January 9th - January 20th. A faculty meeting was held on January 10th. Ms. Valdes formally welcomed the teachers back, stressing how much they were appreciated. The 2012 FCAT schedule was distributed to the teachers as well as a sample contract for students performing unsatisfactorily. Ms. Valdes also reminded teachers that they must review the writing results with the students on

January 12th and conduct writing conferences with students. She stressed that fourth, eighth, and tenth grade language arts teachers must develop and implement strategies to use with students scoring under 4.0 on the district writing test. Ms. Valdes reiterated that Ms. King and Ms. Lara would continue to give support to the fourth graders. I informed the teachers that an afterschool program would utilize our facility after school for about four weeks, and it was important to make sure that classrooms were locked after leaving them. It was also an opportunity for us to recruit students for the following year. The most effective method of recruitment for Lawrence Academy had been word of mouth. I shared with them that we had steadily increased in overall population over the past five years in the three schools, and we hoped we could continue to do so with the elementary keeping on track. For a brief moment, I could see the level of anxiety increase by the expression of the teachers when I made the last statement. I quickly reminded them that they were doing a great job and they had a great principal. Undoubtedly, the resources that were accessible to them were second to none. The meeting was adjourned at 4:30 p.m. Teachers had begun to stay a little later because, not only was the third nine-week period ending the following week, but we were planning collectively to make sure that students would get the most out of the next two to three months.

Ms. Valdes and I had a phone conference immediately after the faculty meeting with our new attorney for the renewal process for the elementary school. The meeting with the district was scheduled for February 2nd. Ms. Valdes and I had already submitted the documents that he requested. He told us there should not have been a revision to Lawrence Academy's contract in the informal hearing that was held on June 16, 2011 to change the contract from a ten year to a four year, provided that the elementary school did not improve. Our new attorney went on to explain that even though the governing board chair was represented, Lawrence Academy did not have legal representation.

"It is not illegal, but it is highly unethical, considering the severe consequences," he told us. Lawrence Academy is essentially fighting two major battles at once, one to improve the school grade and the other to renew the contract. No one is going to care about the time and energy it took to build what is indisputably unprecedented or what has been accomplished at Lawrence Academy if the grade does not improve." The lawyer continued, "I know that your students were not hand-picked and your goal is to promote the importance of a community school. This is all water under the bridge, and I am confident that we will be able to pull this off successfully. We have to show without a doubt that our students are going to be successful on the 2012 FCAT 2.0," Attorney Dotson concluded.

Our attorney said we needed to be precise in addressing with data the issues that were addressed by the CSO in the charter school, renewal document. Mr. Katz and I had given Ms. Valdes the previous data on the school and she was able to address the issues that were raised by integrating the past data with the present. As Ms. Valdes addressed some of the questions posed by the attorney, I drifted into my own little world. For the first time since the inception of the school, I felt helpless, and that I had absolutely no control over what was going to happen. I had a front row seat in experiencing firsthand all those postulates that I learned about this "educational mammoth." The district had been supportive of charter schools, and particularly small charter schools that focused on preventing students from falling through the cracks, but as the numbers began to dramatically increase, a silent war was emerging. The district sent a memorandum to all regional superintendents and all principals on June 23, 2010 entitled "Student Reverse Recruitment Plan." The deputy superintendent presented a major initiative to recruit students that were in charter schools. The writing was on the wall, but I, along with our Governing Board, did not adequately plan for a legal war with the district and definitely not with the state. The importance of lining up a political strategy beginning with a hired lobbyist in Tallahassee was becoming crystal clear to me. But the realization was too late for us at this time in which the majority of our investment had gone into securing a new facility.

The phone conference continued for about ten more minutes, and I was not in the mood for any further discussion. I could see Ms. Valdes was not either. We just quietly packed up our belongings. I went to pick up Michael from the after school program, and I did not make any stops or detours on the way home. The ride home felt more exhausting and endless than usual.

The only saving grace to conclude the week was the three-day weekend. My husband and a few select parents had organized our students to be in the Martin Luther King Parade in Florida City on January 15th. The cub and Boy Scouts were marching in front of two cars with our elementary, middle, and high school king and queen. I decided not to go to the parade so that I could just get time to relax and enjoy the kids. I did exactly that. My husband arrived home around 5:00 p.m. and briefed me on everything that occurred. He enjoyed it as well as the kids, and numerous pictures were taken. His pleasure with the outcome of Lawrence Academy's participation was reassuring; a positive impact was made on the community.

## 2012: January 16-22
## (Dr. Martin Luther King's Birthday)

On Monday, January 16th, the day Dr. Martin Luther King's birthday was formally observed, we played monopoly, our kids' favorite game. As we were playing, I could not banish the image of a young African-American on the news responding that Martin Luther King had done a lot for the African-American community, like freeing the slaves. He was almost 100 years off target between the events of slavery and the civil rights movement. Michael and I took the time to talk about why we celebrate Martin Luther King's birthday. On the following day, I shared the information with my social studies teachers and instructed them to utilize the activities on the district's social science website to address issues of history sequencing, and to examine the contributions of Martin Luther King. This made me more aware that many of our students' poor general writing skills had more to do with a limited knowledge base than the mechanics of writing. The teachers as well as their support team had dramatically helped the 4th graders to improve their mechanics, but there was little that could be done in a short time to broaden their knowledge base, and nothing could be done about the limited life experiences. Many of them considered going to Miami as a major trip outside of Florida City.

The teachers, with the assistance of the reading coaches, conducted data chats in reading, math, and science based on the winter interim assessment data on January 17$^{th}$-18$^{th}$. Ms. Valdes shared the results with Ms. King and me, highlighting that 71 percent of the students who increased their reading skills since the fall interim and 77 percent who improved in math. The most impressive data was our third graders, the students that had been with us since kindergarten. They had the highest rate and the highest percent correct on the winter interim, both in math and reading. The pattern was clear, with the current six graders who attended Lawrence Academy two or more years, with 69 percent of them making high standards/learning in math and 63 percent in reading when the FCAT 2010 was compared to the FCAT 2011. It became evident that the longer a student matriculated at Lawrence Academy, the greater the likelihood the student would increase his/her performance. This did not deviate much from my 1996 dissertation that, outside of social and economic background, students can significantly increase their likelihood of the student academic achievement if the school could cultivate a level of self-efficacy through competent teachers and individualized learning. It was also evident with constant changes in the state's accountability standards; it would be more difficult for a school with an at-risk population to reach any level of proficiency because of the implicit rules governing the normal distribution curve.

When data is presented as reliable and valid from the state, no one wants to think otherwise. I received a firsthand lesson that laws do not follow rules for statistical reliability when the number for each cohort at each grade level decreased from twenty-nine students to ten students for grading purposes in 2010. My decisions to accept students from other nearby failing charters hedged on the very fact that Lawrence Academy would not be graded based on a sample size less than statisticians recommend for reliability, therefore, giving Lawrence Academy time to work with the students. My gut wrenching survival mode entertained "kicking" out the lowest performing grade level of students, but my sense of decency would not allow it. What long term impact could that have on an individual being exited from school to school? Being the mother of a child with a learning disability made me even more aware of the heightened sensitivity among students that have academic challenges. In my 25+ years in education, I had never heard a child say he/she did not want to learn.

"Keitha, Ileana, with our new attorney we are going to have to make sure all our bases are covered and that we have ample data to back up our claims," Ms. King said.

I quickly replied, "I think that Ms. Valdes and Mr. Katz have done a great job with putting that together. Another issue I am extremely concerned about is the paper trail for our ESE students. We all know now that Ms. Grambling has not properly documented the ESE and the ELL population. This is clearly unacceptable for someone with twelve years of experience. Our handicap is that we needed her to be the expert because of our limitations and she didn't do that."

"Well, I know ESE is my weakness, but we have made sure that our students are being serviced," Ms. Valdes followed.

"That's good enough for us, Ileana, but you know that if it is not properly documented, it doesn't count," I replied.

Ms. King said, "Keitha, I think you made the right decision to give her two weeks' notice. She did not teach one class, and her responsibility was to make sure that we were in compliance. Ileana, I'm glad you contacted someone from the district for the new candidate."

"It is amazing how people can present themselves in an interview. I remember in the interview I made it clear that this one was one of the areas in which we needed the most help, and she is getting her doctorate in that area," Ms. Valdes said.

"Case in point, ladies. I am not going to be at the meeting scheduled for the morning of the 31st to review what is going to be said in the meeting on February 2nd. I have a doctor's appointment. I have faith in the students, teachers, the administration, and everything is going to be fine. Just wait and see."

## 2012: January 23-29
## (A Little Time for our Seniors)

Monday, January 23rd was a teacher planning day. The teachers had the morning to complete grades. A brief meeting was scheduled after lunch for teachers to update their Individual Professional Development Plan (IPDPs) and Mrs. Valdes and Mr. Katz reviewed them. Also, the teachers were instructed to begin the Progress Monitoring Plans (PMPs) and complete them by the 31st.

The seniors had their first major event on January 25th after weeks of fundraising. They had a picnic in the park with catered food and a range of planned fun and games. Mr. Katz chaperoned the trip with the senior teachers and a couple of the parents. The senior class was proving themselves to be more independent by their level of responsibility and their ability to follow through. This was a dramatic change over the years. Many of the students had been with us since the 6th grade. The elementary school had taken so much of our time that we sometimes overlooked the significance of the transformation of our seniors, the product which showcased our efforts.

## 2012: January 30-31
## (More assessments and
## Preparation for the Renewal)

The third grade portfolios were due on the 30th. Ms. Clayton ensured the assessments were administered and graded. Letters went home to parents at the end of the month for the PMPs and the status of the portfolios. Parent conferences were scheduled as needed.

Ms. Valdes, Mr. Katz and I met to review the schedule for February that would lead up to testing and the renewal meeting that we had with the district. Mr. Katz had assisted in helping us to prepare for the district meeting on February 1, particularly with the data. Most of the meeting was routine. Early release and the teacher planning day would strictly be used for teacher planning and the department chairs would oversee the needs of their departments.

## 2012: February 1-5 (The Renewal Meeting)

On February 1, Ms. Valdes, Mr. Katz, Ms. King, our attorney, his assistant and I had one final review via phone conference before the meeting. Since it was early release, Ms. Valdes and Mr. Katz met at the school to oversee early dismissal. Our meeting was scheduled at 1:30 p.m. and we decided to meet thirty minutes before the meeting. Initially, Mr. Hunter, our accountant from Tallahassee, was not going to be able to make it, but he was able to rearrange his schedule. He knew that everything was critical in this hearing. On my way to the school board building, I picked up Ms. King. Outside of room 559, there was a sense of uneasiness that had not been present in previous meetings. I had begun to not only know theoretically how bureaucracies operate by rules, guidelines, and procedures, but I began to see the operation up close. As the number of charter schools began to increase, the level of impersonality began to increase. The meeting was delayed, which was not unusual. We were greeted by one CSO representative around 2:00 p.m. The Executive Director of Charter Schools called the meeting to order. Everyone introduced him/herself. Immediately, one of the charter school's supervisors began to highlight the deficiencies of Lawrence Academy Elementary, which were all related to substandard performance based on federal and state guidelines. In spite of the fact that our attorney, as well as Ms. Valdes, could more than adequately support the worthiness of Lawrence Academy's proposal for renewal with the following information, I felt that a pre-determined decision had been made.

# Historical Overview of Elementary Population

**2008-2009**: Opened with 30 students

**2009-2010**: One hundred thirty disadvantaged students added following the closure of nearby closed charter.

**2010-2011**: Sixteen additional students accepted.

Current Enrollment: 176 students

Population Growth: Nearly 600% over 4 years.

- 60% of students had not attended a pre-school program.
- 99% of students received free/reduced lunch.
- 70% of students were siblings or relatives of middle and senior high students
- Average classroom size =18 students
- 52% Hispanic, 45% Black, 3% Other (one of the most diverse charters in the county)

## 2009-2010

- Renovated existing facility with new classrooms to accommodate new students
- Hired a paraprofessional for K-3
- Hired a part-time counselor
- Provided classroom libraries, computers and other learning aids in each classroom
- Provided educational fieldtrips incorporated in curriculum
- Provided educational competitions and clubs
- Provided Saturday tutoring in math, reading and science

## 2010-2011

- Hired new assistant principal, reading coach and two part-time interventionists.
- All teachers attended all required district professional development workshops and other workshops in areas of need.
- An additional 25 computers were made available in the cafeteria.
- Smart-boards were purchased for all science classrooms.
- After-school tutoring was added twice a week (in addition to Saturdays 2011-2012)

## 2011-2012

- Moved into new state-of-the art school building
- Hired full-time Principal
- Hired full-time SPED/ELL Specialist
- Hired full-time Reading Coach
- Hired one reading and one math interventionist
- Maintained at least four student computers in each class
- Increased after school and Saturday tutoring
- Maintained a Computer Lab with thirty computers
- Opened a Media Center with a Media Specialist
- Increased the fidelity of FCIM

This information was followed by the better than average performance of our 3rd graders, which was the only group that was enrolled at Lawrence Academy since kindergarten. The third graders that had been with Lawrence Academy had a proficiency rate of 57 percent in reading with an average percent of 70 percent on the winter interim compared to 0 percent proficiency with those that had been with us one year with an average of 58 percent correct; however, 80 percent of these students showed progress from the baseline. Similarly, those third graders that had been with Lawrence Academy less than one year had a proficiency rate of 38 percent with an average of 56 percent correct; however, 100 percent showed progress from the baseline. A similar pattern was presented in math.

Even though Mr. Katz was not directly associated with the elementary school, he worked closely with the elementary school at various levels since Lawrence Academy, Inc. was a small organization. It appeared that Mr. Katz rubbed one of the panelists the wrong way when he was speaking on behalf of the elementary school. With graph visuals, Mr. Katz pointed out that the current sixth graders that had matriculated at the elementary school and attended Lawrence Academy for at least two years (69 percent of the students in math and 63 percent of the students in reading) had made learning gains.

In all of the district findings, Lawrence Academy presented compelling evidence to show the systematic steps that had been taken to address the findings, such as documentation to show:

- All teachers were highly qualified with the exception of one teacher who did not have ESOL endorsement
- All grade levels had made improvements over the baseline scores
- Numerous support such as Gizmos, Ticket to Read, Brainchild, FCAT Explorer, Accelerated Reader, and Reading Plus
- Parent surveys were completed and the community involvement specialist had been following up with the requests on the survey

- Active Parent Task Force had over twenty meetings and scheduled activities since August

The committee addressed Lawrence Academy's special education services, primarily the inadequacy of the proper documentation. Even though our students were being serviced, the complexity of the paperwork had not only left us out of compliance, but perhaps most of the district in one way or another. Lawrence Academy was under the radar. In my estimation, the releasing of our specialist was just a scratch on the surface in the larger scheme of things related to special education.

The only area with no findings was financial management. The audited financial statements of Lawrence Academy did not identify any deficiencies in internal control over financial reporting of revenues, expenses, and fixed assets and, the school had complied with state mandated quarterly reporting, and continued to be in good financial standing.

I felt that before the decision was rendered not to renew Lawrence Academy, a set of procedures and guidelines were rigidly followed without consideration that we had been the most successful in bringing a community together, and the school was steadily growing as well as the performance. We tried to show that it is almost statistically impossible to make drastic changes when the standards have been changing every year since the school was accountable to receive the grade. However, this did not resonate with the committee. It did not matter that Lawrence Academy didn't resort to methods of data manipulation such as "cherry picking" students or exiting students before the second FTE so they would not be calculated in the grade. My saving grace was always reflecting on the foundation of any school making every attempt to stay on course with the vision and mission of the school. Nevertheless, the reality was that educational policy did not always effectively address educational issues.

The assistant superintendent and the director of charter schools had privately met with Ms. King and me about a month prior to this meeting and essentially stated what the gist of the meeting would be. The only concession would be that they would reinstate our original charter provided Lawrence Academy made the grade in spite of the fact that test standards had changed every year Lawrence Academy Elementary was in existence, unlike the middle and high school that had more years behind them. We could not get this agreement in writing, although it was promised to us in the June informal hearing.

The most unsettling aspect of the entire meeting was at the point when Ms. Valdes broke down toward the end of her presentation. I could only shed tears as she explained the consistent effort she had exerted to make a difference in scores with the communal support of everyone involved. I know from our perspective, "Ileana" was quite effective. She was always up past midnight examining data and making sure that differentiated groups were in line with the benchmarks the students needed to improve. We convened "data chats" well past school hours and made all of the adjustments she suggested based on the data. I made sure the resources were in place to make it happen. As I gazed over the faces of the panel, not one of them was remotely moved by what was presented. It was perhaps business as usual from their perspective. I have strong feelings about what happened in that room, and my feelings are reflected in the two political cartoons appearing below on the following pages.

**Political Cartoon I**: After the renewal contract meeting, my feelings led to the development of this cartoon. As a public servant, it is difficult at times to accept that values such as commitment, service, and dedication are irrelevant in the scheme of things when circumstances can create legitimate reasons to not be in alignment with statutes and guidelines.

Copyright © 2015 (Original concept by Keitha Burnett and illustrated by Rafael Matigulin)

**Political Cartoon II:** The sign reads, "I'm for all Children." Indpt. (Independent) Charter. This political cartoon depicts the obstacles independent charters as a "stand alone" entity may encounter. To my thinking, if independent charters have community support and corporate (professional management company), there will be a greater probability of reducing issues related to conflicts with the sponsors and to some degree issues related to educational accountability.

When the vote was taken, all but one voted to reject our renewal. In the private meeting, the assistant superintendent stated they would revisit the case after the grade was released, but in the formal meeting, it was not stated. We were told that we could present our case to the school board that would be held on April 18th, and we immediately informed them that we would be present.

Our usual routine after district meetings was to debrief at some local restaurant, but the meeting ended a little late, and we did not want to run into the afternoon traffic. Nevertheless, Ms. King and I had a long ride home to discuss not only every aspect of the meeting, but also the broader issues surrounding our decision to remain an independent charter after our accreditation.

"Keitha, all of us have done the best we know how, and it's not like we have infinite lists of support, or at least a list that counts to get us where we need to be."

"I think my dreams were too big when you look at the reality of our community and I just got caught up in believing that if other students can have the best of the best, why can't my kids?"

"There's nothing wrong with the dream," Mrs. King said. "Your dreams just preceded the laws that needed to be in place to protect your vision. It's in God's hands."

"In the business of education, it's not easy making the best decision, "I said. "Dr. Lewis always told me I needed to consider a management company, but all the negative articles on the front page news made it difficult to move in that direction." On the other side, the district had no vested interest in helping us. In the original contract, it did not state that the district "must" close a school after two consecutive years of unsatisfactory academic progress, it says, "may."

"You can't continue to stress yourself out about things that are said and done and things you do not have control over. After you have done your best, you have to learn to let go."

"Ms. King, I know that you're right, but it just takes years of deprogramming. I grew up believing that if you work hard enough, good things will come. I will never forget when one of my first students gave me a scenario many years ago. He said, "You can be driving along in your car thinking that you are in total control, and in just an instant, you run over a big rock in the road, then you totally lose control of the car. That's how life can be."

Now the big lesson switches to how you deal with your circumstances.

The following day was a teacher's planning day. Everyone wanted to know how the meeting went. I tried to present it positively, and stated simply that we just have to continue what we are doing.

And that is exactly what we did. We did our regular tutorials and Boy Scout meetings on Saturday. February 4th. Business as usual.

## 2012: February 6-12
## (Intervention, Reinforcement,
## and more Reinforcement)

The Voyager schedule was updated to reflect the smaller group sizes and the new locations. The reading labs continued every Tuesday and Thursday after school. The after school program, sponsored by The Children's Trust, was still operating Monday through Friday from 3:30 p.m. to 6:00 p.m. every day for grades 4-5. Students had the opportunity to work on their homework assignments and, academic computer programs such as Brainchild and Reading Plus.

The coaches' meeting was held February 6th was and was presided over by Ms. Valdes. She reviewed academic concerns, potential RTI, grouping of students, intervention schedules, Voyager, bi-weekly exams, lowest 25 percent reading and math. On February 7th, a faculty meeting addressed FCAT Prep/ Crunch time, discipline concerns, technology issues, and writing across the curriculum.

## 2012: February 13-19
## (Proficiency trumps Valentine's Day
## and Black History Month)

The week was uneventful other than Valentine flowers sold during the week and the Valentine Party held on Friday, February 18th. Black history activities were incorporated in the lesson plans, primarily through language arts and social studies. I gave all social studies teachers the activities that were on the district website. The students, teachers, staff, and administration were very focused on getting students proficient, or at least improving, on all of the standards. The teachers involved in the writing test were trained during this week. The Saturday tutoring continued as scheduled.

## 2012: February 20-29 (Days Before the FCAT Writing Assessment)

President's Day was February 20th which gave everyone a break before the first major standardized testing, writing for 4th, 8th, and 10th grades. Following the holiday was a faculty meeting with the same topics as the previous week. At this time, the escalating tension was evident as the FCAT writing date drew near. The stakes were high, and everyone knew that the very existence of Lawrence Academy weighed solely on the students' performance. The teachers as well as students looked stoic. To humanize the irrational side of the educational process, Mr. Katz, Ms. Valdes, and I planned a black history luncheon on February 23rd. Teachers were treated to a dinner catered from a local barbecue restaurant. For the students, the caterer prepared a special black history lunch. The students were asked to bring a dessert that could be found on almost every traditional African-American table, for Sunday dinner such as chocolate cake, pineapple cake, sweet potato pie, banana pudding, apple or peach cobbler. It was a nice diversion that did not change or alter the school day.

February 28th was the big day. Teachers and students were told to arrive thirty minutes earlier than usual. We wanted them to have the opportunity to eat breakfast and have some time to mentally prepare for the testing process. All the students were in first period by 8:20 a.m. Testing and non-testing students were in assigned rooms by 8:35 a.m. We made sure that no more than twelve students were assigned to a familiar classroom with a familiar teacher. Representatives from the district were there by 8:00 a.m. to monitor the test. Coffee and muffins were in the workroom for them upon their arrival. Even though any testing is stressful, it went smoothly without any hiccups. Across the school, there were only two students that missed the test. The make-up days were scheduled on February 29th and March 1st.

After testing was complete, the teachers at the high school and middle felt more confident than the elementary teachers that proctored the exams, based on the time on task and the students' composure. At this point, it was a "wait and see" process, and as my mother would say, "time will tell all." Besides, this was just the beginning of the convoluted testing roller coaster.

## 2012: March 1-4 (The Parent Task Force)

On March 2nd, the Parent Task Force meeting was held. Ms. Scott highlighted the importance of students attending all of the available tutorials that were being provided by the school, and the importance of students reading at least thirty minutes a day for elementary school and forty-five minutes a day for middle and high school. As Ms. Scott repeated the directions in Spanish, Ms. Watts passed out the tutorial and the testing schedule to the parents. She also passed out a list of activities that would be closing out the school year.

While the Parent Task Force was having their meeting, the Boy Scouts were being honored by the mayor and the board of commissioners for their volunteer work with the Environmentally Endangered Lands (EEL) Program. The Boy Scouts had religiously kept the property adjacent to the school clean. The wooded area was on the endangered lands list. I had taken a tour on the land earlier in the year. A county worker showed me all of the exotic plants that were now endangered. I felt proud that my husband and the scouts were making a significant contribution. That evening, our family went to our favorite restaurant and a movie for some needed quality time with the kids.

## 2012: March 5-11
## (Preparation for CELLA Testing, Title 1 Audit, Mock FCAT 2.0 Testing, and Senior Activities)

The testing window for the Comprehensive English Language Learning Assessment (CELLA) was scheduled for March 5th through April 4th. CELLA measures the growth of students that are English Language Learners in mastering listening, speaking, reading, and writing skills in English. Ms. Valdes, Mr. Katz, and I met on March 6th to review the items that needed to be addressed at the faculty meeting. With the end of the year drawing near, it was important for us to review ethics/professionalism, child abuse reporting, photocopying, and detention schedule. The end of the year can always leave doors open for crisis level issues if potential issues are not addressed, particularly before all the standardized tests are administered. After testing, administrators, teachers and students are all more susceptible to letting their guard down.

While we were meeting, Ms. Scott met with Title 1 for the annual school audit. From time to time, Ms. Valdes and Mr. Katz were pulled from the meeting to address some required questions. There were no major issues or concerns raised, which enabled us to complete our meeting, and after school the faculty meeting went smoothly.

Ms. Scott had a busy week. She scheduled a parental portal workshop at 9 a.m. on Wednesday to train parents on how to use the system. Only about ten parents showed up, but we were elated to have the ten. The senior picnic was on Thursday, followed by the senior parent meeting on Friday. The senior meeting was to address the final activities and expenses for year.

We had a school-wide Mock FCAT 2.0 test on March 8th for the purpose of giving us more information on what standards we needed to focus on during and after Spring Break. We scheduled three days for the elementary school students to come in during the break specifically to cover testing strategies and to work on specific skills from the Spring Break packet. Ms. Valdes had targeted the fourth graders, who had shown the least improvement based on the last interim testing. On March 9th, Ms. Valdes, along with the reading coach, Ms. Lara, updated the pullout schedule.

On Saturday, some of our high school students took the SAT at a local high school and the Boy Scouts sold camp cards at Publix for one of their fundraising activities. Ms. Lara, and Mr. and Mrs. Cruz volunteered to assist with tutoring during the spring break in math and reading. After the spring break tutorial, my family took a mini-vacation to the Keys. On March 27th-30th, I was scheduled to go to Bogota, Columbia to observe an individualized model of learning sponsored by a local non-profit organization. I was excited about the opportunity.

## 2012: March 12-18 (Turbo Tutorials)

Spring break was March 12th-March 16th and students were scheduled to return on Monday, March 20th. On Monday, Tuesday, and Wednesday, an average of twenty students attended tutoring, and we picked up several students to ensure they would be present. The teachers reviewed test strategies followed by one hour of math and one hour of reading. The teachers used a combination of the Spring Break packet, web-based programs and interactive activities to guide their instruction. Ms. Valdes kept a log to reward the students with a certificate and a gift card for the end of the year. In the meantime, the teachers rewarded students with stickers, candy, and praise.

After the tutorial, everyone took a mini-vacation before returning on Monday. It was going to be a stretch before the end of the year and there was a lot to be done.

## 2012: March 19-25 (School Lockdown)

Monday morning was difficult, as expected, after a break, but with everyone knowing the importance of "time on task," the teachers focused on honing in on the skills in which the data revealed the students were deficient. The coaches reviewed the data which showed how well the third graders, the students that started with us in the kindergarten, were performing. We had our scheduled faculty meeting on March 20th, which was a follow-up from the items on the February 21st meeting. Ms. Scott continued to hold the Parent Portal workshop every Tuesday throughout the month of March. She recruited some teachers and parents to attend the District Advisory Council (D.A.C.) on Thursday evening. On Friday, Ms. Barrios' class had won the pasta dinner by raising the most money for the *Lymphoma Pasta for Pennies* and the seniors held their senior dinner at Red Lobster later that evening.

Ms. LaCount and I sponsored a Lock-in for success. Fourteen students attended from Friday evening to Saturday morning. Several of them only attended the evening activities and went home afterwards. Ms. LaCount and I brought our daughters, hoping they could benefit from the activities as well. With a tight schedule of activities including reading and math activities geared to test-taking strategies, along with food and movies, the students crashed by midnight. With blankets and sleeping bags, the girls slept in the science room and the boys slept in the library. I propped the door open in the library so that I could check on them. My office was directly across from the library, and I had a couple of the books that were on my "to read" list. I was ready for an all-nighter. Melanie slept on the couch in my office while I sat at my desk as the designated "night watchman." Melanie and I had some time to talk and just enjoy one another. She had planned on being a "night watchman" with me, but she soon fell asleep. The night was pretty much quiet until around 2:00 a.m. or 3:00 a.m. when a student came to my office complaining that her back was hurting from sleeping on the floor. I had Melanie slide down, so that she could be at one end and Melanie at the other. She was content, and I decided to check in on Ms. LaCount and the girls. She too had not gone to sleep, and she let me know everything was fine. The boys appeared not to have moved an inch. I think they were just that tired.

I went to the office and continued reading one of Dr. Stanley's series of books. Like a school-aged child, I lay my head on the desk and dozed off around 4:00 a.m. or so. I woke up around 7:00 a.m. Ms. LaCount woke up students and monitored them as they brushed their teeth and got dressed. I went to the cafeteria to microwave the ready-made pancakes and sausages. Melanie came down early, and I had her place plates, cups, napkins and utensils on the table. She also placed the cereal, juice, and milk on the table.

Ms. LaCount and the students were downstairs by 8:00 a.m. I was amazed at how much the kids were eating. Then again, they were growing kids. Ms. Valdes and the tutors came in around 8:30 a.m. to set up for the Saturday tutoring. Students started to come around a few minutes later and they joined the students that had spent the night. We touched base with Ms. Valdes to brief her on the material that we were able to cover. It was not long before other students began to fill the cafeteria for reading and math tutorials. This was a signal for us to exit. We were exhausted!

## 2012: March 26-30 (Trip to Bogota, Columbia)

On Monday, I did not go to work. I had to get ready for my trip to Bogota, Columbia to observe individualized learning that turned around some failing schools. Since the non-profit organization was paying for the trip, I had nothing to lose. Thursday, March 29th, was the end of the term and Friday,

March 30$^{th}$ was a teaching planning day. Ms. Scott was scheduled to provide the parental portal training, and the Boy Scouts
were scheduled for an Advancement Weekend to earn some
badges.

Michael dropped me off early Tuesday morning at the airport.
With international flights, I had to be there two hours before
departure. I had a little time to spare, so I got a cup of coffee
and a muffin before I headed to the gate. Shortly after I arrived, I met the director of the non-profit sponsoring the trip.
She introduced me to a principal of a local charter school that
was also going on the trip. We talked a bit and got a chance
to know one another before we landed in Bogota. After going
through customs, the director led us to her contact who took
us to the hotel. Even though I had four years of Spanish in high
school, and two in college, I could not speak Spanish; however,
I had a moderate grasp of the written language, and I could
comprehend just a little. After we arrived, we had time to get
settled and rest.

Later that evening, we went to the founding school where this
revolutionary individualized learning pedagogy had been implemented. It was stated that this pedagogy is an avenue to turn
a failing school around and make successful schools better. We
had the opportunity to meet the founder. He gave us an overview of the history and the pedagogy. Educators guide students,
allowing them to be the main drivers of their own learning process. With the award-winning FRE pedagogy model, each student is assessed on their knowledge, interests and abilities and
given a personalized learning plan based on that assessment,
allowing them to work according to their own unique learning rhythm. The individualized plan and relational learning

method engage students, who find meaning in their education and do not drop out of school. Students must achieve excellence on every topic, thus no student fails the year. FRE creates an environment that allows students to work with their educator one-on-one.

The energizing aspect of the presentation was that the approach was reminiscent of the vision of one of my mentors, Jackie, who was the founder of a successful design and architecture magnet. The essence of the model was designed to meet each student's need through a process of assessing where the students are and where they need to be based on their knowledge, abilities, style of learning and interests. The steps included starting/ending points, research, skill development and relating.

Over the course of two days, we visited several schools where the goal was to move each student from the guided level to autonomous. There were no strict guidelines in regard to the amount of time a student must be in a given course. Each student works from his/her individualized learning plan. No one could argue with the philosophy or concept behind the model; however, in our state, as in most other states, lesson plans are generally dictated by pacing guides to cover the standards, but they did reiterate that the process can be modified to meet the state guidelines. It was something to consider, but the model would be difficult to implement in the United States if the approach continues to be traditional.

## 2012: April 2-8 (Countdown Begins!!)

Monday, April 2nd marked the month for the countdown to the most significant test in the history of Lawrence Academy Elementary. Even though it was not spoken, it would be difficult for the other two schools to survive without the elementary because of the cost of the move to the new facility. There were enough nerves to go around. I used Columbian coffee that I had a purchased during my trip to make fresh coffee for the teachers in the teacher's lounge. I had spoken with Ms. Valdes the day before, and she thought it would be nice to have pastries to go with the coffee. We wanted to do all those little things to let the teachers know they are appreciated. The robust smell of coffee and the sweet smell of pastries pleasantly greeted teachers once they entered the door.

On a lighter note, Ms. Scott ended the Domino Pizza cards sales on April 2nd. The majority of the cards were sold by the elementary students. The FAIR testing, an assessment system that provides teachers screening, diagnostic, and progress monitoring information for all students that scored a level 1 or a level 2 in reading was scheduled from April 4th - May 23rd. It was difficult to think about any other type of testing that needed to be done when the high stakes FCAT testing was less than a week away.

Friday, April 6th was a teacher's planning day. Most of the teachers' used it as an opt day or as one of their furlough days. The teachers needed a mini-break. There were less than two before testing. In spite of a needed breather for everyone, tutoring was still held on Saturday.

# April 9-15
# (In the Midst of Testing and Monitoring…
# A PREP Rally)

The window for the FCAT Retakes for the high school students was April 8th - April 20th. There was an EESAC meeting held after school on April 9th. The EESAC committee reviewed the bylaws, minutes, roster, end of the year review for the school improvement plan, and the progress of FCIM and RtI monitoring. The Sanford Achievement Test was scheduled on March 10th through March 13th.

The faculty meeting held on April 10th addressed the class failures, the FCAT 2.0 schedule, test taking strategies, the importance of getting both plenty of sleep the night before the test and a good breakfast. All teachers were instructed that all classrooms had to be test-ready by Wednesday, April 11th with all class walls covered, and desks aligned in rows facing the board/clock. All staff must be present by 7:45 a.m. After the overview was given by Ms. Valdes, the test chairs, Ms. Davis and Ms. Perez-Fernandez, proceeded to present a Power Point presentation for the formal FCAT training.

In the midst of all of the preparation for the FCAT 2.0, the one highlight of the week was the "PREP RALLY". There was one given for each school. The elementary was in the morning, and the middle and high schools were in the afternoon. Our guests were body builders. They visited local schools throughout the county and paraded their strength by breaking not only traditional boards, but also bats. At the end, we correlated the ability to tackle difficult tasks such as the FCAT by concentrating as these men did before attempting to break a board or a bat. We also played competitive games with the students with FCAT-like questions and skills, and the winners were awarded prizes. We had the step team conclude the "PREP RALLY" with one of their routines. We accomplished our goal as the students exited the rally on a positive and high note. FCAT was the following week.

As the students poured in for the last Saturday tutoring, the Parent Task Force had a meeting on Saturday, April 14th at 10:30 a.m. Ms. Scott reviewed the parent portal and her availability to train any parent on how to use it. She also made available to the parents downloadable workshops geared to FCAT. The dates of the senior activities were given and the total amount of money rose from the fundraisers.

On Saturday and Sunday evening, I was busy composing my appeal to the school board to repeal the recommendation to proceed with the closing of Lawrence Academy in the event that the school failed to make the grade. A nearby county had granted a charter with two consecutive failing grades to remain open because they serviced an at-risk population, but they acknowledged other significant factors, such as the overall progress of the school. I could only hope that my message would resonate with the board. After numerous trial runs with my husband and kids as the audience, and conferring with Mr. Katz and Ms. Valdes, I was set for Wednesday, April 18th. Even though I would have loved the support of my team at the meeting, they needed to be at the school site even more.

# 2012: April 16-22 (Could it be a Set-up?)

Early Monday morning, everyone was in place to begin the week with the most significant test that would determine the fate of Lawrence Academy Elementary. The district representatives that were monitoring the test were there by 8:00 a.m. Senior class activities were scheduled outside of the building for the entire week, not only to celebrate their "rites of passage" but to minimize any unnecessary distractions. Ms. King arrived early to assist with the testing process. The first day of testing went smoothly, and the newly installed intercom system facilitated the process.

I did not report to school on the following day. My administrative team and Ms. King had everything under control. I needed to practice to make sure that my speech resonated with the school board. Our attorney informed me that he would have his assistant meet me at the school board building for moral support, but he would have to leave by 6:00 p.m. My husband had his own responsibilities at his job, and he was needed to pick up our kids after school and make sure they ate and did their homework. This was not my first time venturing out alone. The first time was the presentation of the application to start the middle school charter.

As promised, our attorney's assistant met me at the entrance of the school board at 12:30 p.m., and we sat in the far right-hand side of the school board auditorium. As usual, there were many presentations and items on the agenda. It was nice to see many students being lauded for their many accomplishments. It reminded of me when my students were recognized by the school board in the late 1980s for winning the state championship in the Black History and Culture Brain Bowl. My students were recipients of four-year college scholarships; and to this day, I am still in contact with most of them. They have done exceptionally well in life. At 5:00 p.m., our agenda item had not come up. I had acclimated to the environment and actually felt comfortable after sitting there for so long. I assured our attorney's assistant that I would be able to handle it alone. I called my husband to let him know I was fine. He had picked up the kids and ordered pizza. I was not surprised. In spite of my strenuous schedule, I did take the time to make sure my family had well-balanced healthy meals, and I took pride in that as my mother had before me.

The school board meetings were always long and at times intense. One item that heated up on the agenda was a local charter school that was recommended for closure. The alleged case against them was they were using a shed for one of their classrooms, and that the facility was used to host adult parties. I was more focused on my presentation which was on the next item agenda. Toward the end of the drama, the executive director of Charter School Operations came to the back of auditorium and I knew it was time for me to present.

As I was about to rise she said, "On no, Dr. Burnett, it's not time. As a matter of fact, they are going to break for about thirty minutes or so. You can go and take a break and I will make sure you aren't skipped. I know you have been here since this afternoon."

"Are you sure it will not be a problem?"

"No, I am going to be here. You don't have to worry," she said reassuringly.

I thought about it momentarily and agreed that it would be good to stretch before I gave my appeal to the school board. I went to the restroom to freshen up and the assistant superintendent for school choice was at the sink. Appearing a bit shaken up, with her hands raised over the sink she stated, "Look at me, I am still nervous!"

Knowing that it was more of a rhetorical statement, it took me by surprise and I didn't say anything, partly because I didn't know what to say, and partly because she left abruptly. I quickly freshened up and stepped outside just to compose myself and rehearse my lines. I quietly returned to the back of the auditorium, feeling confident that my appeal would resonate with the board. Enough time and energy had been spent in the preparation. I continued to sit patiently anticipating speakers for Lawrence Academy to be called. Glancing at the agenda, it appeared that they had skipped around. After thirty minutes or so, the executive director of charter school operations approached the back of the auditorium in my direction and I knew it was time for me. Picking up my purse and portfolio, I started preparing for my walk to the podium.

"Dr. Burnett, you weren't in the auditorium and they proceeded."

"What are you talking about? You specifically told me before I left that it would take at least thirty minutes and I know I was gone not even half that time."

"I knew you didn't want to follow that group. Your case is no way near theirs. It is late and you can do your presentation next board meeting in May. I will make sure of that," the director stated emphatically.

I didn't know what to make of this, but my head was spinning. "So, no action was taken?"

"Don't worry about it. You will have the same opportunity next month."

After the director returned to her seat, I called my attorney's assistant and informed him of what had occurred. He told me first and foremost to drive home safely. He added that it was a little surprising that they would do that, but not off the radar. "We can have a phone conference first thing in the morning with Attorney Dotson and me. I will brief him on what has occurred, and we will go from there. Don't worry about it at this point, and just be safe driving home."

I felt better, but not relieved. It was well past 9:00 p.m., and it was unnerving just to think that I had sat there for nearly nine hours. I had practiced my three minute presentation more times than I cared to think about or mention. As I drove home, I could not resist stopping by the nearest Starbucks drive-thru for my comfort drink, a grande cappuccino with four raw sugars topped with whipped cream, but I also wanted a large chocolate chip cookie. I used my last inch of willpower to successfully withstand the urge for the large chocolate chip cookie.

As I took my first sip, I could begin to feel the release of stress as I focused more on the satisfying taste of my sweet, smooth, and creamy cappuccino. I was home within 45 minutes and everyone was asleep. Just for now, I did not have to share what had happened with Michael. A good night's sleep would definitely give me a better perspective of what occurred.

After barely having a quick breakfast with Michael and recapping the previous night, my cell phone had racked up five missed calls. Michael asked me more than ten times as to why no one at the school was with me and eventually he finally understood that every "body" was needed in the building. With the district overseeing the test, there was no room for any mistakes. In the midst of a chaotic morning, little Michael and I left almost an hour early. When we arrived, Ms. Valdes and Mr. Katz were already there.

"Did you read the paper?" Ms. Valdes and Mr. Katz said almost simultaneously.

"What are you talking about?"

Placing the paper in front of me, I read the article about the school board voting to close the charter school that allegedly had been throwing parties and having students in a shed. It also reported that the school board voted to close Lawrence Academy Elementary. There was no separation of the issues from one another. It was apparent to me that the executive director acted to protect the interest of the district, or at least her boss that was so visibly upset, and did not want to hear the testimony of another charter school. I was denied the opportunity to speak.

"Listen, I have a conference call with the attorney in about an hour or so," I told Ms. Valdes. "Don't worry about it. Just make sure everything goes well with testing, and reassure the teachers that everything is fine." Just say at this time, it is not accurate." While Little Michael went to the cafeteria, I went to my office to begin damage control.

I began to review the procedures for school closure. The law clearly states that a school district "may" close a charter school if it does not meet the stated requirements which are academic and financial. A nearby school district had elected to keep a charter school open after it did not meet the academic requirements because the board took in consideration the challenges of the school and the strides that had been made. We had an increased enrollment, a viable middle and high school, a new state of art facility, and a sound curriculum with multi-level support. There was also a clause which stated the district had to give a 90 day notice before they could terminate a contract.

Ms. King entered my office that morning, but not with her usual "cheerleader" greeting. From her expression, I knew she had read the article.

"Keitha, what happened? Why didn't the newspaper comment on anything you said in your presentation to the board?"

"I didn't present. At the time I was to present, "you know who" came personally over to my seat to tell me the school board was taking a break for 30 minutes or so and cajoling me to do the same since I had been there so long. You know the rest."

"It is evident that it does not matter how much progress has been made, and that time has proven to be an asset to Lawrence Academy. I bet while you were out, they hurried back in place and got the vote through. My goodness, I know how hard you practiced."

"Ms. King, we don't have the tools to beat this Goliath. Let me call the attorney and see what he has to say."

After a lengthy conference with the attorney and his assistant, they assured us this was protocol for them to have everything in place in the event we do not improve on this FCAT. I understood what they were saying, but I truly felt my freedom of speech had been intentionally circumvented. We went back and forth on the legality of what occurred. Essentially the attorney stated the time and effort would not be worth it because the executive director could easily deny she told me to take a break. They stated it would be better to handle this internally.

"Keitha, think about it. If she went that far to have you not to speak, what makes you think she would voluntarily confess to what she did?" added Ms. King.

I could not argue with what they stated. The best thing I could do was to focus on what was going on in the school building. There were too many irons in the fire. I immediately drafted a letter to all parents of the elementary to address any rumors they may have heard. Ms. King and I drafted the letter below to all parents.

Dear Parents:

This is a letter to inform all parents that Lawrence Academy Elementary currently must improve on the 2012 FCAT or there is a possibility that our charter will not be renewed. The Lawrence Academy Governing Board, the Director, administration, faculty and staff are all confident that our students were adequately prepared and there is no need for alarm. They have an excellent principal, Ms. Ileana Valdes, highly qualified teachers, adequate books and supplies, and pullouts/ tutorials sessions. We believe this is our moment of FAITH and as always, we ask for your support.

For rumor control, please fill out the information below and have your child return it to his/her homeroom teacher. If you have any questions, please call Ms. Valdes at (305) 247-xxx or Dr. Burnett at (305) 281-xxxx.

Most parents returned the forms the next day and Ms. Valdes and I received phone calls to soothe parents' fears. The seniors continued their level of excitement with their planned activities for the week. The presentation that I did not have a chance to give haunted me for months.

The text of my presentation is as follows:

Superintendent, honorable school board members. My name is Keitha Burnett. I was recruited from North Carolina in 1985 to teach in this district and I have taught in some of your most challenging schools as well as some of the most prestigious. I enjoyed some of my greatest successes as well as some of my greatest challenges. As a national board certified teacher, I was honored to teach in one of the most progressive school districts in the country and I felt it was an honor in 2005 to have the opportunity to open a charter school in the name of my parents that would service traditionally non-college track students by giving them the tools and encouragement to attend a postsecondary institution. We offer a solid curriculum, wide range of activities and supportive services for our population and our middle and high schools students have shown some of the highest gains in the county and approximately 70 percent of our seniors will be attending a postsecondary institution this year. With our goal to supplement the school district by focusing on the average to below average students, I felt very comfortable with you as our sponsor.

I am standing before you this evening because our elementary school, the newest addition to our Lawrence Academy family, has struggled with the standards for primarily two reasons: the elementary is relatively new and secondly, the standards have changed each year we have been accountable. I know there may be legislation that would possibly increase the number of years a school has to improve, but time is running out for us. It is evident that we have a track record for improvement and we have invested in providing a state-of-art facility for our students. As policy-makers, I know you understand the complexity of educating our most vulnerable students and the need to have commitment which we have shown over the past six years. I am most humbly soliciting your support this evening to not vote at this time to proceed with the steps to close Lawrence Academy Elementary where we build the character of tomorrow's leaders.

# 2012: April 23-30 (Winding Down)

After the last day of testing, we held a faculty meeting, April 24th. A number of items were addressed. Ms. Valdes reminded everyone about the state visit on May 7th. The Department Heads presented the standards in reading, writing, math, and science which needed to be included in the summer assignments along with a strategic plan to improve our math and reading programs. The final weeks for the elementary would focus on skill-building, with the kindergarteners and first graders focusing on SAT skills, second graders on FCAT, third graders on writing and fourth graders on science. The end-of-course dates for geometry, biology, algebra, and U.S. History were given.

Teachers were given the intent to return forms that were to be returned by the end of the week. They were also and reminded about the importance in keeping discipline in check by continuing to have structured lessons. Progress reports were scheduled to be distributed on May 3rd. The full schedule of activities for all three schools was also distributed. With the elementary, middle and high school, there was almost an event for every day until the close of school. In spite of the tenseness of the next state visit, the district presence during testing or the constant pendulum hanging over our heads, the teachers were just as excited as the kids about the upcoming events.

On April 26th, I returned to school for the governing board meeting at 7:00 p.m. and the meeting started at 7:20 p.m. The minutes of the last meeting were read and approved. The final budget was tabled for the June meeting to include adjustments. I gave the Director's report which included most of the items that occurred at the faculty meeting on the 24th. Ms. King encouraged all members to attend the events. A presentation was given to the board by a Fontan Relational Education representative, on a pedagogy based on individualized learning. The governing board did not vote to support the program at this time, but would consider it at a later time. The governing board voted to approve adding the Enrichment Center. Ms. King informed the board that a letter sent home to that referenced the closure of the elementary and the preparation for the 2012-2013 school year was in process. There would be a summer program for third through fifth grade. The meeting was adjourned at 8:45 p.m., and the date for the meeting in June was left open until further notice.

The seniors left for their mini-cruise to the Bahamas on Friday, and were scheduled to return on Monday. From the comments of the students, it was indeed a once in a lifetime opportunity for them that would forever be part of their "happy bank" of memories. All of the elementary students spent a much deserved day at the zoo.

The homeroom teachers had begun collecting drinks and non-perishable desserts for Family Day, a day of food, fun, and activities in the park.

## 2012: May 1-6 (Family Time)

Outside of early release on May 3rd and the Parent Task Force on May 5th, the week was uneventful; which was great for our family. The kids got a chance to make a cake for their Dad's birthday, and Michael and I got a chance for dinner on Miami Beach.

## 2012: May 7-13
## (Not a State Visit, but a Fieldtrip to the Library)

The much anticipated state visit did not occur. Instead, Ms. Valdes just had to send in the report . At this point, it was safe to assume that everyone was waiting for test scores. We had made a significant stride in offering advanced placement classes in biology, Spanish, and Language Arts, which were scheduled that week. Ms. Scott scheduled an EESAC meeting on May 9th at 4:30 p.m. to address some of the final issues for the closing of the school. The faculty meeting scheduled for May 8th was brief which reiterated items from the April 24th meeting. On May 9th, my son and I left to take a train ride to my hometown to de-stress, spend some time with family, and to make time for me to work with Michael on some of his skills.

The kindergarteners and first grades students took a trip to the library on May 10th, with bag lunches in the park afterwards. The teachers told me when I returned that the students en-joyed the story time and wee excited by the opportunity to get library cards. In 2012, it was hard to believe that the majority of these students had not been inside of a library.

## 2012: May 14-20 (Activities for the Soul)

The End-of-Course (E.O.C.) Algebra was scheduled for the window of May 14th through May 18th. On May 15th and 16th,

a local non-profit agency provided a two day teen empowerment workshop for our high school students. It was a great opportunity for students to hear the life challenges of successful
people as give them well as the opportunity for them to discuss
tough teen issues such as abuse. Lawrence Academy had been a
partner with this organization for the past two years. In previous years, they had provided teen empowerment workshops,
healthy relationships curriculum, and two cruises to promote
family unity. The students received perks such as "dress for success outfits".

I missed my first Family Day for the elementary on May 17th.
Michael and I returned the night of the 17th from our trip. Mr.
Katz and Ms. Valdes made sure that the Lawrence Academy
tradition of family, fun, food, and organized activities for the
entire day happened. On the following day, I was back for the
middle and high school Family Day. They had the extra treat
of having a DJ, who was one of Lawrence Academy's former
students, who would be graduating from vocational school.
Everyone was so proud of him. He was one those students who
would have easily fallen through the cracks. With repeated failures, he was ready to drop out. His mother and I had both
agreed he needed an alternative program where he would be
around older students. Neither of us were willing to give up
on him. I referred the mother to a nearby charter that had
a partnership with Job Corps and this was where he'd found
his success. The success was evident in his maturity and the
presence of confidence. This was a landmark trait of Lawrence
Academy's approach to education.

The teachers added a special touch with each class designing
their own t-shirts. After the games, I left early to get ready for

the bridal party that I was hosting for my niece, Kisha, which was scheduled at 2:00 p.m. the following day.

## 2012: May 21-27 (It's All About Family)

An EESAC meeting was held on Tuesday, May 22nd to complete all unfinished business from the meeting held on May 9th related to the school's corrective plan.

There were two major events on Friday, May 25th, the eighth grade dinner and dance, and the Orlando trip sponsored by a local non-profit organization. I did not attend the eighth grade dinner and dance since I was one of the chaperones for the Orlando trip sponsored by the same non-profit that sponsored our teen summit. This trip was a family mentoring trip with workshops and activities designed for building strong families. My husband and I decided that we would attend as chaperones and bring our kids. The great part about this trip was parents had to participate, involving them in the experience, and making the trip much easier to handle. We left the school around 5:00 p.m. There were about 13 families representing our school. We stopped to pick up about 5 families representing a school on the north end of the city. There was no room to spare with two representatives from the sponsoring agency and the additional school. It did not take long for Melanie and Michael to find a companion for the trip.

The trip was relaxing, and we stopped only once near the halfway marker to Orlando. Michael and I talked the entire trip. When we arrived at our destination, we were pleasantly surprised that our stay was at a five-star villa resort. We stayed on board the bus until the agency's representative returned with the keys and the family mentoring t-shirts. Michael and I helped to distribute the keys and the t-shirts to the head of each family. The representative reminded us of the first meeting on Saturday morning which would start at 8:30 a.m. There were two families in each villa, with the exception of our villa, which was the central meeting place for our school. It was almost eleven o'clock before we were able to settle into our rooms. Our villa had three bedrooms with a large living room area, dining room, and a full kitchen. We had scheduled a movie in our room at 12:00 midnight. Most of the families came with pillows, blankets, and snacks to enjoy the movie. It was a pleasure to see parents and kids alike enjoy themselves. I think that everyone left our villa 2:00 a.m.

We didn't go to bed until around three. When the alarm sounded at 7:00 a.m. it was difficult to get up, but I managed to call all the families to remind everyone that the meeting started at 8:30 a.m. They had delivered muffins, juice, fruit and cereal to each room.

Once we arrived, the day was filled with quality non-stop family building activities. Some of the more interesting activities were participating in the competitive games and designing a flag with our designated tribes. There were activities catered to different age groups. Mike and I attended a workshop on developing stronger marriages that was facilitated by the founder of the organization. It was informative and interactive. There were more activities after lunch, and the day ended with a barbecue. By the end of the day, everyone was totally wiped out, and needless to say, we took a more than a deserved nap.

The following day was just as hectic. There was a nice semi-formal luncheon at which winning tribes in the competitive games and other activities were recognized. We were entertained with the talents of the students. It is amazing how quickly the students were able to come together to display their talents of skits, dancing, singing, poetry recitation, and rapping in an organized format. The buffet spread of meats, salads, vegetables, breads, and desserts was more than enough to satisfy the hungry appetites in the hall.

Already packed as instructed, we boarded the bus to return home within an hour. The excitement of the weekend delightfully carried over onto the bus. This was an indication that everyone had an excellent time. We made the usual pit-stop at the half-way marker, and we were at the school by 5:00 p.m. We did not have to wait as long as usual because most parents drove their cars and left them at the school. We were able to leave by 5:30 p.m., and it was a great relief there was no school the following day.

## 2012: May 28-31 (Kindergarten Graduation)

School was closed to recognize Memorial Day. This was a relaxing day for us to recuperate from a delightful, but hectic weekend. The major event closing the month was the kindergarten graduation that was held the late morning of May 31st. The cafeteria was standing room only. Ms. Washington and Ms. Steele did an excellent job with the program. It made me think of the first kindergarten graduation that was only three short years before. After the students received their certificates, and special awards and kindergarten souvenirs were distributed, numerous pictures were taken, and cake and punch were served. As we had anticipated, most parents wanted to check their child out of school to spend the day with them. We had the attendance clerk and the registrar help with the early dismissals.

# 2012: June 1-10
# (End of School Activities, A Surprise Teacher's Confession, and Ending with a World-Class Graduation 2012)

The first day of June was the scheduled with the 5th grade lunch and dance and the Senior Prom. I helped Ms. Thomas with the events. While the students were having dinner, I organized the activities for after lunch. I had a former student who was now in his first year of college as the guest speaker. He pitched in to help decorate the cafeteria. When the students arrived, we had place settings for each student, and I complimented them on their outfits and congratulated them on their efforts this past year as well as their teacher, Ms. Thomas who had planned the activities. I introduced them to a very special person that had attended our school five years ago and was now in college. The most important element, Erick, was from the community. He briefly spoke to them on the importance of education, the difficulties he had, and how hard work helped him to overcome most of his adversities. He cheered them on and told them the importance of having dreams and goals to get there. Erick resonated with the students because he was still young and he was one of them. He hung around a while to chat with them and take pictures. The DJ started playing music, and the 5th grade party had formally begun. We had various desserts to cap off the full-course meal the students had eaten at local restaurant. Ms. Valdes socialized with the students for a while, but she had to leave because she was going to attend the senior prom along with Mr. Katz. The dance was scheduled to last until five, but most parents picked the students up directly after school. Ms. Thomas had several high school volunteers to help clean the cafeteria and arrange the tables back into place. I stayed around with Ms. Thomas until all of the students had been picked up, and, shortly thereafter, I went to pick Michael up after school. I thanked Ms. Thomas again for a job well done and both of us were on our way.

On Monday, we had our major awards assembly for the elementary scheduled at the community center. Our cafeteria could not accommodate all of the students and parents. After the students had lunch, we bused them to the community center. Mr. Katz set up the award table and the microphone and the Parent Task Force set up the refreshment table. As the parents began to come in, Ms. Scott had them sign the roster and the ushers passed out programs. With Ms. Valdes serving as the emcee, she gave the grade level teacher, the responsibility of presenting their awards. The special guests of the morning were the eighth graders, dressed in blue and white. They marched in to their front row seats. There were the traditional academic, attendance, and citizenship awards, but the special awards that became a part of Lawrence Academy Awards Assembly were the Character Awards. Homeroom teachers gave a unique positive attribute of each student based on the premise that every student has a positive attribute. Another special award was in the name of the founding governing board chair, the late Mr. Pearson. The recipient of this award was a student who was recognized for honor, integrity, self-determination, discipline and high academic standards. The last recognition was a framed inspiration poem given to every eighth grader with a graduation medallion. The afternoon could not end without recognizing the teachers with certificates for their hard work and dedication. Mrs. Valdes also announced the $3^{rd}$ grade scores in math and reading. The third graders had been with us since they were kindergarteners. As I looked over the audience, in spite of the great scores, it felt a little eerie, as if this was the last time we would meet as a school. Even the fact Ms. Valdes and I had received phone calls "off the record" from individuals in the district giving their support was not enough to soothe this uneasiness. By the time cookies and punch were served, we were on schedule and it was time for students to board the bus to return to school. The teachers passed the flyer I made to each student as well as a summer camp flyer for incoming 3-5th graders (Appendix A). The scores of the third graders were phenomenal.

The remaining four days were early release. We had a brief faculty meeting on Tuesday with closing of school issues and concerns. After the meeting, I had an unusual visit from Dr. Middlebrooks. Dr. Middlebrooks had been diagnosed with scleroderma, an auto-immune deficiency that results in the hardening and tightening of skin, and as a result, I had to demote her from her position as elementary assistant principal to lead teacher for the middle and class teacher because of the stressful demands that were associated with the elementary. She was doing a great job, and her students had improved an average of ten percent based on the interim assessments.

"Dr. Burnett, I just want to tell you how much I appreciate you and what you have tried to do for this community. I am from this community, and I know it is difficult. I mean I really admire you. I can tell you that you may be the only charter school that tries to give all students a chance to succeed."

"Dr. Middlebrooks, thanks, and you know I would do only what my parents would have done. And I want to say to you that you really have grown so much over the past three years and I appreciate all you have done for these kids. You have really proven yourself."

"I am going to tell you the truth. I was really angry with you when you demoted me, but I got over it because I know and now believe you made the right decision, and I got through it, and I really do enjoy it. I was so mad at the time. With my illness, I have learned what is important in life and most of all, who my true friends are in this world and I have found out they are few. It is as if I can see from a different set of lenses and see the world for what it really is." With tears in her eyes, and a wavering voice, she said, "It's one thing to have friends to turn their backs on you and say cruel things about it, but when it's a close family member, it's unbearable."

Nearly a year ago, she had shared with me that she had been diagnosed with scleroderma, a rare auto-immune disease that affects the body by hardening connective tissue that supports the skin and internal organs. This affects African-Americans more severely than whites. "Dr. Middlebrooks, you have to understand that you can't take on the worries of the world and what is important is that you focus on you and get better."

"I know, but the reason I came to see was not to talk about me. You know this disease has humbled me, and I just think people don't really see what I now see in you. I don't think they see the work and sacrifice you are doing in this community." Simultaneously nodding my head and moving my hands to embrace her hands. Her words moved me and I could not help to feel that she was telling me much more than the conversation at hand.

On Wednesday morning, the middle and high school students also had their awards assembly at the local community center with the same format as the elementary school. The elementary parental attendance was by far greater than the middle and high school parents. After the students were dismissed early, the Parent Task Force sponsored their annual luncheon for teachers and staff at a nearby restaurant nearby. As usual, Ms. Scott, with a few parents, worked very hard to sponsor this event each year.

On June 7 at 6 p.m., our senior class had beautifully decorated the cafeteria for their first capping ceremony. The concept behind the capping ceremony is to allow each student to be represented with a person they consider to be his/her greatest support. I found it interesting Elver Salgado was the platform speaker for the class, because he resisted and at times rebelled against what we were trying to accomplish at Lawrence Academy. He has allowed me to print his speech below:

Good evening ladies and gentlemen. Thank you for joining us in our capping ceremony. It really means a lot to us for you all to be here. My name is Elver Salgado and I am a senior that will be graduating tomorrow. I come from a migrant family where education is a serious issue. Both of my parents didn't finish school because of the financial situation they were in, and they fought hard to come to this country. They came to this country in search of the American dream everyone was talking about. Their minds were set to find work and a better way of life for me. It brings joy to me to say that after 13 years of hard work and dedication, yes that includes kindergarten, I am finally going to bring home my high school diploma. Bringing home my diploma really means a lot to my father, because I did what he always dreamed of doing. I know he's proud of me and I'm overwhelmed. I am the first in my family to receive a high school diploma, and I am a first generation college-bound student. For some students, getting a diploma is nothing too important, but for students like me, it has been a great obstacle for me to overcome. See in the 9th grade, I had a GPA 0.8, but thanks to my mom who always told me "Hechale ganas, sino vas a terminar trabajando Como you en el so!" Her words motivated me to do my best and thanks to the support of my teachers, I am able to get my diploma tomorrow.

I remember in the 11th grade Mrs. Hawkins called my mom because I wasn't doing my work, and although I was punished, I can say thank you to her because she put me on track to do my work and her dedication paid off.

I would like to thank my parents for bringing me to this world and giving me the opportunity to have a great education. Also, I would like to thank Dr. Burnett and Mr. Katz for allowing me to be part of this wonderful family, which is Lawrence Academy, I want to say thanks to all my friends that since middle school we still stick together and to the friends I met this year. Last, a special thanks to Becky and Ana because they were there to comfort me at a time when the world around me was crashing down, and they taught me to have Faith and hope in God.

My fellow seniors, the advice I want to leave planted in your heart is "Don't screw up an opportunity when it presents itself." Keep that in mind and once that opportunity presents itself give it your best shot!

Well friends, family, and staff, take a good look at this group of seniors. In here, there are doctors, lawyers, officers, and I know that we have proven to the world that we indeed have the character to be the leaders of tomorrow.

"Oh my goodness, Elver gets it....gratitude, growth, faith, hope and vision," I thought to myself. I had to find him at the end and let him know how proud I was of him. I did not know there were so many people attending until the end when everyone was taking pictures or enjoying refreshments. Eventually, I did get a moment to give him a hug, and I told him that my mom would have been proud of him too. I think Lawrence Academy capped off the evening quite well.

Outside of the teacher planning day and grades due by noon, our graduation was scheduled at the Cultural Arts Center on June 8 at 3:30 p.m. Most seniors and teachers were there by 2:30 p.m. The programs were elegantly done with the crest on the front. We started about five minutes late because one student was missing. Ms. King was a stickler about the graduation starting on time, and rightfully so. As we began to march in, she showed up and managed to get into formation before we entered the center. As we were still standing, Joel presented the flag and led us with the Pledge of Allegiance followed by the national anthem by Reaiah. Ms. King gave the welcome. We had two senior addresses given, one by Rebecca who had been with Lawrence Academy since the 6th grade and Ashley who was the Student Body President. With the permission of Rebecca Sanchez, her graduation address is printed below. I have read the speech over and over since the graduation, but the written words do not express the emotions that surfaced that afternoon. There was not a dry eye in the center. Without a doubt, there was a strong spiritual presence as she spoke.

Good afternoon, parents, family, friends, staff, teachers, and the graduating Class of 2012! It is an honor and a privilege to be here standing before you. My name is Rebecca Sanchez and I am a senior graduating today. Today, I leave behind a legacy, but I'm also prepared to walk today into tomorrow. I am one of a few students that are known as the founding students. Founding students are those who were here since the beginning of Lawrence Academy on August 8, 2005. On that day, I remember walking through the glass door nervous because I didn't know what was in store for me at Lawrence Academy. I was a little girl in the 6th grade with a rolling book bag and my long hair flying everywhere. As the years passed, exciting events happened in all areas of my life. I met new people; I have gained long lasting friendships and also gained a quality education. But today, I am here before you as an empowered young lady.

It's rare to hear students at more populated schools say that they grew as a family. But, I can sincerely say that the class of

2012 grew as a family. Thanks to Dr. Burnett, who believed that family was such an important aspect in our lives that she made that gateway possible for us. We have seen each other for more than four years, and it's going to be tough starting on Monday knowing that I will not be seeing you as often. Every school year, we would come back to talk about our summer and how they went, but not this year. As we graduate today, things will be different now.

Seniors, we anticipated this day like a young child waits for the day of his birthday party to come. Freshman year came; we thought we were the bomb! Sophomore year came and already seniori-tis was kicking in. During junior year, we just wanted to finish high school and get it over with. When senior year came, we all thought we would each have a smooth year, but when we got our schedules, we found out that we were each placed into about 4 or more Advanced Placement classes. It was tough, but well worth the effort!!

I hope that you all enjoyed the activities that we did this year. And although you all could be knuckle heads at times and a great headache, I must thank you because through you, God taught me how to be humble and how to remain humble. There is something about each of you that I have learned throughout the years. You have played an important role in the forming of my life.

Now that we began a new chapter in our lives, we have to be prepared for what the world has to offer. Battles and obstacles will come as we leave today because the majority of them are there to make us mature and grow. But when the battles do present themselves, it's up to you to decide how long you will stay on the ground. I encourage you to get up as soon as you can because time will pass and by the time you know it, you will be behind on many things. I once heard from through a cancer survivor, that one way to cope with pain, distress, and hardship is to laugh your way through and make the most of life. I also want to challenge you to never give up when the world around you is crashing down. Don't get stuck in pointless foolishness, and if you find your way out, learn from it. Don't forget to just sit back and relax at times and enjoy quality time with your friends and family. And I hope that one day; you may all get to find out the true reason you were created to live.

As to the teachers, I want to thank you because school was like our second home, and you all were always there looking out for us!

I would like to thank Dr. Burnett for being a woman of such dedication, support and love for her baby eagles that are mature and ready to fly today.

Although she is not here, and is a former teacher, I would like to thank Ms. Betancourt because she was like a big sister that I looked up to for all the years that she was here.

To Ms. Vargas, after having a long day at work, our 8th period talks and seeing you smile brought a smile to my face and made my day.

To Mrs. Hawkins for being like a mother to me; thank you for your guidance, support and comfort when I needed it.

I appreciate you all dearly. And you all have left not just memories, but foot prints in my life.

Above all the people there are to thank, I must thank God who has brought me up to this moment. If it weren't for Him, I wouldn't be here today. I also want to thank my mom and family for being so supportive and a great help through all these years. I hope that I have made you proud!! And also, to my dearest friends, Juana, Abigail, Anahy, and Bobby, that have been there for me, thank you!

Last but not least, seniors, take challenges, take risks!! Experience different adventures! Be the best at what you want to be and be happy today and every day to come! Don't forget to give back to your community. And never forget who you are and who you want to be! And I wish you all the best in life! Congratulations CLASS of 2012!! I love you all! God Bless You!! Thank you!

Becky received a standing ovation, making it difficult for the guest speaker to follow. The guest speaker was the CEO of a local nonprofit organization that provided services to our students. She had worked for a Fortune 500 company, but left to start a nonprofit that focused on providing educational services geared to at-risk students. She reflected on growing up poor in a South American country, but having a desire to do better and give back to those that are less fortunate.

I followed the speaker and gave a brief reflection on each one of the graduates for the purpose of letting them know that I personally "knew" who they were and ended with Mother Teresa's poem, "Do Good Anyway." I had used this poem many times for awards ceremonies and presentations, but this time when I read the line, "What you spend years building, someone can destroy overnight. Build anyway," it felt prophetic, and a tear rolled down my face as I read it. As I took my seat and listened to Reaiah's original song she composed especially for her class-mates as the video was shown that had captured highlights of the Class of 2012, I could not get that passage of the poem out of my mind. At the same time, my husband had his own personal struggle as the county was dismantling the Head Start Program and awarding contracts to public and private agen-cies to take on the responsibility of providing the service. He had worked as a Center Director for the past ten years. Even though he was confident that he would be placed within the county, he really enjoyed working with the population he was serving, which was similar to Lawrence's Academy's popula-tion. Since there were few male role models in early education, the kids, including our students that were Boy Scouts, looked up to him. Our vision was to eventually combine forces and provide a comprehensive educational program in one location that would incorporate the Head Start Program. We knew it was critical for us if we were going to be successful with our population. For now, it was just wait and see.

Mr. Katz presented the Class of 2012 and Ms. Perez-Fernandez called the names as each one was formally recognized by the receiving line that included Mr. Katz, Ms. King, Ms. Valdes, the guest speaker, and I. We had invited the district to take part of this momentous occasion, but there were no representatives. I had been a part in many ceremonies, and I would definitely say the quality of the program ranked in the top ten percent. As everyone parted with congratulatory hugs and kisses, it marked the last of the one hundred and eighty days for the seniors, but the fate of the elementary school now rested on the state's final tally sheet of points to calculate the school grade.

# June 11-August 1 (The Verdict)

In spite of the possibility that Lawrence Academy Elementary might cease to exist, we continued, with the advice of our legal counsel to operate as if the school was going to open in the fall. We held a summer camp for grades 2-6 from June 18th-July 31st for academic, recreational, and social enrichment from 8:30 a.m.-3:30 p.m. To cut back on cost, I served as the administrator from June 18 to the first week of July and Ms. Valdes and Mr. Katz rotated for the remaining days of July. The raw scores had come by the end of June, but the grades had not been calculated, and the formula had constantly been changing.

With my urging, Ms. King and I met with one of the largest management companies just to explore some of our eleventh hour options. I had considered a management company, but because of reservations, I never followed through. A representative of the company and one of their principals came to the meeting. After hearing our story, he quickly called one of his connections to ask whether they had an "open elementary charter" available. This is where I begin to understand and see that it is not always hard work, due diligence and a strong work ethic that pays off, but knowing how to maneuver in a system and that is what independent charters like us lacked. Unfortunately, the "open charter" had expired. He explained to us that they could have had our parents transfer the students to the "open elementary charter"(charter that has not been used) and our students could remain where they were just by getting a change of location of the "open elementary charter" to Lawrence Academy. He made it clear that the district would not have liked it, but they could not do anything legally. The representative told us that he thought we made a great business decision to move to the new facility, and if we had a different population, the outcome would probably be different. Just by the fact that we started with the middle school, he felt that we were serious about trying to make a change in education.

This was an eye-opener for both Ms. King and I. Our perspective had come from the original purpose of charter schools to serve as an educational supplement to districts by providing a small school setting for students that may have otherwise fallen through the cracks. The district was still seen as a partner in our efforts, but as the district begin losing record numbers of students, the role of sponsorship had become more complex. Just the previous year, as I had stated, the district sent a memo to all principals to actively recruit back all students that had left public schools to charters, yet charter schools were not given the same information to recruit from public schools. It was evident organizations behave in a manner to maximize their chance of survival, but I had never envisioned education institutions behaving as such. In our minds, perhaps we should have invested in a management company in our earlier years in spite of the negative press, but hindsight is always 20/20. We had survived the 2008-2009 downturn in revenue for education, but now our hopes were now limited to the final results of the FCAT 2.0 scores.

In the meantime, I needed a break from all of this. My family had planned a two week road trip to visit family, attend the family reunion and attend my niece's wedding starting the week of August 9. Halfway to our destination, I received a phone call that my brother was very ill and probably would not live more than two days. We took a detour from our intended destination to be with him. It was a difficult time for me, but for the first time during Lawrence Academy's existence, it really didn't matter to me or it just didn't register in the forefront of my mind. I later found out that our attorney sent an appeal correspondence to the district in the event Lawrence Academy did not make the grade, one dated July 10 (Appendix B), the second one on July 12 (Appendix C), and the third one on July 16 (Appendix D). During this time, Lawrence Academy Elementary had been highlighted in the news for one of two schools in the county with the highest learning gains. The district officially sent a letter to Ms. Valdes and Ms. King on the 18th to give them instructions for the school closure process, but I was unaware of this at the time. Ms. Valdes, Mr. Katz, and Ms. King decided not to inform me about the outcome at the time. In spite of the unprecedented learning gains, Lawrence Academy Elementary was less than 20 points shy of passing. We did not make it.

In the state's convoluted grading system, I did not understand how a concession could be made that no school could not drop down more than two letters grades; however, no concessions were made for schools that were failing and dramatically increased, but missed the targeted passing rate. Additionally, the grading system was not approved until midway through the school year. The representative from the large management company shared with Ms. King and I that they could have easily lobbied for that concession because it made perfect sense, or should it be political sense? Regardless, it was a whirlwind that literally took us by storm. The closing of the elementary had a detrimental impact on the remaining two schools, primarily because of the loss of FTE dollars (Political Cartoon III).

Ironically, my brother did not die within two days, but on August 9th, the first week of school that Lawrence Academy opened its doors, perhaps serving as a progenitor of the fate for the Lawrence Academy Middle and Senior High.

Copyright © 2015. (Original concept are by Keitha Burnett and illustrated by Rafael Matigulin).

**Political Cartoon III**: With the closing of the elementary school, nearby charters readily accepted the elementary students that scored at proficiency level on the FCAT, and those that did not, were left, even though they had shown improvement. The students that needed the setting of a small school the most, had to return to the traditional school setting. Some charters even accepted elementary students on the condition that their older siblings applied. With less resources, and more students with less ability, and additional standards, it became clearer that the other two schools would have difficulty in succeeding.

# REFLECTION
# AND
# FINAL NOTE

No matter how long the night,
the day is sure to come.
African Proverb

# REFLECTION

The greatest impact on Lawrence Academy Middle and Lawrence Academy Senior was the loss of the elementary school, which made up slightly over half of our total student population. Families were literally broken apart. Lawrence Academy was one of the first charters to embrace a K-12 concept on one campus. Committed to the concept of "free and appropriate" education for all students, Lawrence Academy embraced students from two failing charters that would eventually lead to the demise of the charter during the summer of 2012, in spite of the evidence that the students that started with Lawrence Academy (grade 3) scored above the district and state in math and scored better in reading than all of the surrounding elementary schools.

The near crippling challenge occurred in 2012 after Lawrence Academy, Inc. lost its elementary school (shared facility with the middle and high school), in spite of unprecedented learning gains. Lawrence Academy had been a haven for underachievers and students from two nearby closed charter schools. There had been a strategic investment of resources in terms of time, effort and capital, which made it difficult for the remaining two schools to spring back quickly. Rumors of closure for all the Lawrence schools, and some of the nearby charters reacted to our misfortune by using "predatory" strategies to recruit the best students at our school.

The committed faculty and staff at Lawrence Academy clearly understood the importance of increased accountability in education, but education should take into account that it takes time to make significant change. As I stated earlier, I visited and studied Douglas Preparatory School and the Harlem Kids' Zone in New York before starting this venture. The Harlem Kids' Zone took 30 years in the making. This is one of the reasons why we believe there has been so much controversy concerning the reliability and validity of testing coupled with using one method of performance, particularly when we are attempting to make a significant difference in the lives of at-risk students. Issues such as numerous changes made in testing standards as well as having cohort groups of less than 25 to calculate school grades have left unanswered questions. High-stakes testing clearly is not

One major event that happens in the neediest community is "creaming" even if it is simply based on a student's success on state standardized assessments. He/she may not be the brightest student, but the mere fact that they are able to pass standardized testing makes that student "desirable." Everyone wants the best kids with the least behavior problems, and those are students that are welcomed with opened arms. Even though it may have been to our detriment to a certain extent, we stood by our charter to provide "free and appropriate" education to all students, and we remained committed to targeting students who are average to below average with the intent of increasing the percentage of these students attending college.

Lawrence Academy's greatest achievement has been the graduation rate and the percentage of students that attend a two or four year college in spite of 95 percent of the students receiving free/reduced lunch. In 2013, 76 percent of the students graduated and nearly 60 percent enrolled in college. In 2012, 85 percent graduated and 62 percent enrolled in college and in 2011, 80 percent graduated and 100 percent enrolled in college. The rate includes not only students that started with Lawrence Academy in the ninth grade, but also students that transferred in their junior or senior year, primarily because of issues related to underachievement.

Lawrence Academy's major strength for the most part has been the consistency it has shown in learning gains and the consistency in math by performing higher in math proficiency than the surrounding schools, with the exception of 2013. Nevertheless in 2013, Lawrence Academy Senior performed higher than all of the surrounding charters and traditional schools on the Algebra 1 E.O.C. In 2012, Lawrence Academy sixth and eighth grade performed higher than the majority of the surrounding charter and traditional schools on the math portion of the FCAT 2.0. With nearly 60 percent of the students at the high school level passing Algebra, Lawrence Academy Senior High outperformed all surrounding charter and traditional high schools as well.

With 90 percent of our teachers and staff in tact during the 2013-2014 school year, Lawrence Academy moved to a smaller facility, but a much less desirable site one year after the loss of the elementary. Nevertheless, the facility had a library with 6000 volumes, a student to computer ratio 1:1.5, a cafeteria, two offices, 7 classrooms equipped with restrooms, various educational web-based programs for students, six active clubs. Lawrence Academy also had partnerships with Florida International University Pre-College Program, Florida City Hall, Florida City Plaza, and Kids for Non-Violence Project. Lawrence Academy was successful in renewing its' accreditation fall 2013.

In the report, we stated that within the next three years, Lawrence Academy's goal was to improve the overall proficiency performance in all common core areas, with an emphasis on reading, increase the range of services offered to students through partnerships, and provide more opportunities for activities and enrichment. We knew that in order for Lawrence Academy to remain viable, it was necessary for Lawrence Academy to renew its commitment to academic excellence, refocus efforts to provide extracurricular activities/ electives and recruit more students to provide more resources for the school.

With a surge of new charters and magnet programs within three miles that were drawing our best students, the Governing Board voted to close the school on October 1, 2014 due to under-enrollment. Even though it was a small number of students that left for a new school, it was a large percentage of the population of Lawrence Academy, and without the elementary, there was no longer a feeder pattern. Lawrence Academy already had a plan in action after the closing of the elementary school in 2012. There had been many conversations and meetings that focused on the late founding governing board chair, Mr. Pearson who stated, "As long as the kids are better off, the right decision is being made." In spite of the compassionate plea from students and parents, I still believe our students, based on the last parent meeting, were still better off at the time with us, but with the deteriorating financial outlook, it was no longer true. The parents showed up in record numbers in the cafeteria, but I had seen this before for critical meetings. As soon as the lights are off, the parents went their separate ways. The parents had been unsuccessful in helping in a major meaningful ways such as political and financial support. At the same time, I clearly understood that 'blaming the victim" would not accomplish anything, but we could no long take on the level of insurmountable stress. We could no longer afford to keep Ms. Valdes. Mr. Katz was hospitalized for a stress-related illness in 2013. Ms. King's term as chairman coming to an end and I too began to suffer from stress-related symptoms. I was not only assisting with administration, but also I had a full teaching load since we lost the elementary. All of our teachers taught an additional class and took on some administrative tasks. Contrary to what it should be in a high needs school, our turnover rate was very low, generally 10 percent to 20 percent on a yearly basis. Additionally, the middle school charter was up for renewal. There was an individual from a local non-profit who was approved as a volunteer who was "attempting" to recruit our students for a new charter school. Her efforts were thwarted by an irate parent who contacted me. Our parents were very loyal, but loyalty does not equate to financial support. As a result of the off-the record decisions and actions that were made during the June 16th and the April 18th with the district, there was very little trust in giving the district all the details before it was necessary. Only after there was no concrete resolution from the parents or a viable corporate partnership, the board voted to close the school with a plan that would be in the best interest of the students, faculty, and staff in the long run. We had anticipated that the district would reverse funds for that month, but we were able to make payroll. Until this day, we have not received a reply as to why the last month's funds were not returned to our account since the schools receiving our students did not receive the funds and secondly, there was still unfinished business at Lawrence Academy, such as picking up the assets and closing all business operations. To the very end, students said things to amaze me and that is why I know without a doubt that Lawrence Academy was a special school and the spirit of this school will transcend time. The last student to speak at Lawrence Academy was Stephanie. With her permission, her impromptu speech is printed below:

I am here today so that you guys can see the face of a student seriously being affected by the closing of Lawrence Academy; I am a single teen mother and have gone to too many schools. None have helped me the way that Lawrence Academy has helped me. My first day at Lawrence Academy, I literally felt the stimulation of a real learning environment. I felt like I was truly being academically challenged and I am so heart-broken to hear that it is closing. Thanks to this school, I am graduating a whole year in advance. Lawrence has helped me to get where I am today. No other school would let me stay after school till sometimes seven at night to do virtual school and to get to where I am. It is easy sometimes for teachers to just care about a pay check and getting through the week, but not the teachers here. They show interest and take their time to help their students. The closing of our school could have been prevented if we would have the funding if more people would have taken the time to care.

Some people may wonder as to why I was so committed to a project that seems deemed a failure because of the insurmountable, if not impossible obstacles. Believe me, I thought about abandoning this project many times on many occasions. There was always a haunting spirit that kept me focused on why I had gotten involved in this project in the first place. Should I have expected support from our sponsor or the community as a result of the possible repercussions of having a truly open door policy? In the application for the charter, I had quoted Dr. Mann from Florida Memorial University that had worked in low-income areas who concluded that one of the major problems in low-income areas is the lack of sustained and effective commitment from grassroots organizations on a long-term basis.

Most of all, I could not separate from my own past. I am intrinsically compelled to stand to the end, primarily because of not only my strong religious convictions, but also my personal experiences. I was born 1961 in the segregated rural south in North Carolina. As one of the first groups of students to benefit from the Elementary and Secondary Act of 1965 which provided for the federally funded Head Start Program, a brief interlude of integration was experienced. After Head Start, all the students returned to segregated schools. Schools would not be fully integrated until 1971 after the United States Supreme Court Swann vs. Charlotte Mecklenburg case (1971) which Court upheld busing programs that would speed up the integration process in school districts. I especially, cannot forget those teachers prior to integration that gave me the educational foundation that would give me and countless others the tools to succeed in all environments from undergraduate to graduate.

Had all of my work and that of my supporters been in vain? I could only reflect on the words of the late Mr. Pearson, our first Governing Board Chairman, "We can only do what we can and hope that we made a difference somewhere along the way". I took it a step further and simply asked. Below are reflections of the some of the Lawrence Academy family.

"When I was notified by Dr. Burnett I had been officially hired to work as one of the administrators at Lawrence Academy, I was so ecstatic. The reason I was so thrilled was due to the fact I would be able to work with students who needed the utmost attention and it was a chance I could REALLY make a difference in their lives.

Prior to my first day at the job, I had researched the school's test scores, student achievement rate and the student demographics. I always knew Florida City was one of the poorest cities in the State of Florida, but never realized how these students needed us. Students did not want to be in school. Parental support was minimal.

The staff was one of the best I have worked with during my 24 plus years in the field of education. Some teachers had been there for a few years. They knew exactly what would be expected of them. We had several openings for teachers so we advertised and received dozens of applications. We sifted through them and interviewed the ones that seemed would fit into our school, based on their previous experience and education. At the conclusion of the interviews, we always advised the applicants that this was not just a teaching position; but you had to have the heart, dedication and commitment to making Lawrence Academy succeed. And the teachers did give their

ALL. Every day was a commitment on the teachers and staff's part to make our students learn and build their self- esteem.

Every day I walked into all the classrooms, several times a day, and observed our committed dedicated teachers and staff. Students were eager to learn and having fun in the process. These were students who initially didn't want to be in school, but were now making a connection between what they were learning and applying this to everyday situations.

In December 2011, we were notified the State of Florida was changing the school grading system for the current school year. I did not understand how Florida could change the school grading system in the middle of the school year. You would think the new grading system would be implemented for the following school year. The school grade would be based on a stringent new scale. This would make it extremely difficult for students to show a large amount of student achievement.

I can remember when the first test results were released in March 2012 and our third graders had done an exceptional job. Little by little during the next few months, different tests scores were released. In the end, it would not be enough to have our school stay open.

Six years later, I still think about Lawrence Academy. At least weekly, I often wonder what else we could have done. I think about our students who gained a love for learning, the dedi-cated teachers, the support staff, our clerical staff, our lunch room ladies, our custodians, security monitor, and bus drivers. I also think about the founder of Lawrence Academy, who had a dream to open a school for one of our poorest neighborhoods and always put the students first. Making students always feel they are welcomed, loved, and successful."

Ileana
Former Principal

"Working at Lawrence Academy proved to be a professional and emotional challenge, but I'm grateful for that time. Walking into a school that you know is under the gun and threatened is nerve wracking. Everyone had a sense of insecurity and fear but at the same time determination to give it their all, and that is what they did. I had the opportunity to work alongside some of the most committed and dedicated teachers I have ever met. They knew that every day they were with those students they needed to make a difference and they did. Together as a team we push students beyond their limits and developed a sense of urgency to learn but made it fun. I will never forget teaching a lesson to a class of third graders when the principal came into the room to award them with an ice cream treat at the end of the day for achieving the highest score on an assessment and the students wanted to stay engaged in the lesson instead. They offered to take the ice cream home with them but wanted to finish the lesson first. I couldn't believe it. These were the same students that had such low scores and lack motivation to learn at the beginning of the year. It was all the dedication and hard work that the teachers and staff invested into these students that truly helped them develop a desire to learn and succeed. They worked hard and pushed themselves to the max but unfortunately in a flawed grading system it wasn't enough but for me, we the teachers and staff of Lawrence Academy made a difference."

Aimee
Former Reading Coach

"My name is Tiffany, and I attended Lawrence Academy since kindergarten. Lawrence Academy is and was the best school that I ever attended because the teachers were great and so was the staff. Since the closing of Lawrence Academy, I attended two other schools and I am now homeschooled because there is no other school that teaches character with academic achievement."

Tiffany
Former Student

"Education is the most important thing in a human life because it helps us to evolve into thinkers. To become great at something, it first starts with one thought. Lawrence Academy Charter School was a school that encouraged critical thinking. Both of my children attended Lawrence Academy and I was Treasurer for the Parent Task Force (PTA) alongside Maria Scott President. It was an honor to be part of an exceptional group of teachers, staff and parents. The closing of Lawrence Academy was a lost not only to the students but to the community".

Melissa
Former Parent

"My name is Sumaiya and I was once a student at Lawrence Academy Charter School. My experience at this school was awesome. From the caring teachers to the well mannered students, I've grown to love this school and was upset to hear that it had to close. The memories I've cherished from Lawrence Academy are too many to count on two hands. The teachers at this school were very helpful and understanding. Not only did they teach me, but they turned my learning experience into an adventure, one that I loved. Lawrence Academy has taught me that learning is not always a strain upon children, but is more of a journey, a journey that I will remember for many, many more years to come".

Sumaiya
Former Student

I liked the teachers at Lawrence Academy because they were nice. I learned a lot and was very sad the school closed down. I wish the school could reopen. I had to go to another school and I lost my friends. My mom liked the school because Lawrence Academy is the school that I learned English and my cousins would be in the school now if it was still open.

Evelyn
Former Student

All the analyses and "what ifs" will not bring back the Lawrence Academy we loved and treasured, however, but it is refreshing knowing that celebrities such Lebron James embraced putting "public" back in public schools for "the have-nots." We know that Lawrence Academy was a special place for a season and for that I can say I am eternally grateful. In spite of the final outcome, I know that my parents, the late Mr. and Mrs. Allen and Roxie Lawrence and our first Governing Board Chairperson, the late Mr. Eddie T. Pearson would not want me to look back with regret, but with hope. One of the major purposes of this book is to provide the opportunity and the platform to say to the Lawrence Academy family, "job well done!"

# APPENDICES

# Appendix A

## (Flyer to Parents)

### Lawrence Academy Charter School

*"Building Character of Tomorrow's Leaders"*
713 West Palm Drive
Florida City, Florida 33034
(305) 247-4800 phone
(305) 247-4895 fax

Althea King
Chairperson

Keitha D. Burnett, Ph.D.
Founder/Director

Ms. Ileana Valdes, Elementary Principal
Mr. Israel Katz, Secondary Principal

### Lawrence Academy Elementary School

**Don't Pack Your Bags Too Early!!!**

Congratulations to our students, Principal Ileana Valdes, Teachers Ms. Clayton and Mr. Cruz and our support staff.

#### Released 2012 FCAT 2.0 scores for 3rd Grade

|  | Reading | Math |
|---|---|---|
| **Lawrence Academy Elementary** | **42%** | **77%** |
| Redondo Elementary | 37% | 44% |
| Florida City Elementary | 24% | 49% |
| Laura Saunders Elementary | 29% | 53% |
| Miami Community Charter Elementary | 37% | 34% |
| Campbell Drive Elementary | 25% | 42% |
| Leisure City | 32% | 37% |
| West Homestead Elementary | 30% | 46% |
| Lincoln Marti | 20% | 40% |

# Appendix B

## (July 10, 2012 Letter to the District)

Bilzin Sumberg
ATTORNEYS AT LAW

*Albert E. Dotson, Jr., P.A.*
*Direct Dial: (305) 350-2411*
*Direct Fax: (305) 351-2217*
*Email: adotson@bilzin.com*

July 10, 2012

Melinda L. McNichols, Esquire
Heather Ward, Esquire
Miami-Dade County School Board
1450 N.E. 2nd Avenue, Suite 430
Miami, Florida 33132.

    *Re:    July 2012 Letter from Commissioner of Education Gerard Robinson*

Dear Mses. McNichols and Ward:

    You may already be aware of the referenced letter from the Florida Department of Education Commissioner Gerard Robinson to parents and guardians of students in Florida schools. This letter, coupled with the recently reported comments of Miami-Dade County Public Schools Superintendent, Alberto Carvalho, and Florida Department of Education Vice Chair, Roberto Martinez, provides Lawrence Academy with some concern that, notwithstanding its testing improvement (both as compared to its prior years' testing and its peer schools in the area), a statewide "temporary drop" due to "a number of changes to the State's accountability system have impacted the results" may have unintended and unanticipated consequences to Lawrence Academy.

    When the grades come out, I hope that we can have a discussion about the intent of the Settlement Agreement that we reached since the Florida Department of Education and Miami-Dade County Public School System recognizes that the change this year in the State's accountability system might result in Lawrence Academy's improvement not being fully recognized under the new system.

    We anxiously await the grades and hope that Lawrence Academy's improved testing results will lead to higher grades for Lawrence Academy's elementary school.

Sincerely,

Albert E. Dotson, Jr.

AED/eo\3198925
cc:    Dr. Keitha Burnett
        Mrs. Althea King

# APPENDICES

# FLORIDA DEPARTMENT OF EDUCATION

STATE BOARD OF EDUCATION

KATHLEEN SHANAHAN, *Chair*
ROBERTO MARTÍNEZ, *Vice Chair*
*Members*
SALLY BRADSHAW
GARY CHARTRAND
DR. AKSHAY DESAI
BARBARA S. FEINGOLD
JOHN R. PADGET

Gerard Robinson
Commissioner of Education

July 2012

Dear Parent/Guardian,

By now you have received your child's results on the state-required FCAT and End-of-Course assessments. These assessments serve as annual academic checkups to measure your child's progress in key subject areas and help ensure that your child is on track for college or career.

Florida also uses the results to calculate school grades. Schools that improve a letter grade or earn an A receive additional state funds – up to $100 per student – in recognition of their academic achievement. Struggling schools can get assistance and additional funding – an average of almost $2,000 per student for F schools – to help them improve.

As grades for elementary, middle and many combination schools become available, you may notice that some schools have lower grades than last year. That does not necessarily mean that the schools, teachers or students are not doing as well as they were before. There were a number of changes to the state's accountability system this year that impacted the results.

To help better prepare students for college and careers, the state has been moving to higher academic standards, new assessments that measure students' progress toward meeting the standards, and higher achievement levels for subjects such as reading and math. These new standards, assessments, and achievement levels are being used to determine school grades this year.

Also, Florida received a waiver from the federal government this year that allows the state to have one accountability system instead of two – one state and one federal. The waiver requires Florida to include all students – including those with disabilities and English language learners with at least one year of instruction in the U.S. – in its accountability system.

The combination of changes to Florida's accountability system will cause a temporary drop in some school grades. However, we can also expect student performance to improve as it did in 2007 when Florida made revisions to the school grading formula. At first, the number of A and B schools fell from about 2,000 to 1,952, but, in the two years that followed, A and B schools rose to 2,317.

Each time Florida's school grading system has increased expectations, student performance has improved over time, which is the primary goal of Florida's accountability system. Florida will continue to make the adjustments and investments necessary to ensure all students have the opportunity to get the knowledge and skills they need to be successful in school and beyond.

Please know that, along with the State Board of Education and your district leadership, I am working to make certain that schools and teachers have the resources they need to ensure that your child is getting the best education possible.

Thank you for supporting your child's education.

*Gerard Robinson*

Gerard Robinson

*More information on Florida's school grading system is available at http://schoolgrades.fldoe.org. For questions about school grades, visit www.floridapathtosuccess.org or call 1-866-507-1109. To receive periodic email updates about this topic and related issues, sign up here: http://parents.fldoe.org/home.*

325 W. GAINES STREET • SUITE 1401 • TALLAHASSEE, FL 32399-0400 • (850) 245-0505 • www.fldoe.org

# Appendix C

## (July 12, 2012 Letter to the District)

 Bilzin Sumberg
ATTORNEYS AT LAW

*Albert E. Dotson, Jr., P.A.*
*Direct Dial: (305) 350-2411*
*Direct Fax: (305) 351-2217*
*Email: adotson@bilzin.com*

July 12, 2012

*Via E-Mail and Regular Mail*

Melinda L. McNichols, Esquire
Heather Ward, Esquire
Miami-Dade County School Board
1450 N.E. 2<sup>nd</sup> Avenue, Suite 430
Miami, Florida 33132.

     *Re:   Lawrence Academy Charter School*

Dear Mses. McNichols and Ward:

As you are aware, the Florida Department of Education recently released the letter grades for state elementary schools, and Lawrence Academy was the unfortunate recipient of an "F" grade for the 2011–12 academic year. However, due to the "temporary drop" in scores caused by "a number of changes to the State's accountability system," as explained by Department of Education Commissioner Gerard Robinson in his recent letter to parents, Lawrence Academy's failing letter grade does not at all reflect the dramatic progress it has made over the past year. We sincerely hope that the School Board will consider that clear, quantifiable progress, and not the artificially deflated letter grade, when considering the renewal of Lawrence Academy's charter for the 2012–13 academic year.

Anticipating the decline in grades, the State Board of Education earlier this year voted not to let any school drop more than one letter grade this year. Based on reports, the State Board of Education's decision to blunt the impact of the changes helped nearly 400 schools, of which many would have dropped one additional letter grade without the policy. Therefore, the true drop in grades is not known for Lawrence Academy's peer schools and other schools within the Miami-Dade district -- that did not experience, as Lawrence did, an IMPROVEMENT in test scores.

As compared to its peer schools (Laura C. Saunders Elementary, West Homestead Elementary, and Florida City Elementary), **Lawrence Academy demonstrated *by far* the most progress over the past year.** Lawrence Academy's raw score, used to determine the letter grade, increased by an incredible 25.8 percent from 2011. **During this same time period, the raw scores of many schools, including Florida City Elementary, went *down*,** and others, such as West Homestead or Laura C. Saunders, showed only modest improvement. In addition, Lawrence Academy's numerical score missed the cutoff for a "D" grade by less than ten percent. If it were not for the state-created "temporary drop" in grades that masked Lawrence Academy's

BILZIN SUMBERG BAENA PRICE & AXELROD LLP

1450 Brickell Avenue, 23rd Floor, Miami, FL 33131-3456   Tel 305.374.7580   Fax 305.374.7593

◦ 166 ◦

# APPENDICES

*Melinda L. McNichols, Esquire*
*Heather Ward, Esquire*
*July 12, 2012*
*Page 2*

incredible improvement, Lawrence Academy's letter grade would surely be a "D" or higher, with much higher grades anticipated in the coming years.

**More tellingly, Lawrence Academy's dramatic improvements can be seen in the data for each of the core subject areas.** In Reading, Lawrence Academy performed better than any of its three peer schools, and Lawrence Academy's leap in Science—from 6% to 32% passing (compared, for example, to 17% passing at Laura C. Saunders)—is but an example of the strides that Lawrence Academy will continue to make if permitted to remain open this school year. In fact, the only subject area in which Lawrence Academy failed to defeat or substantially equal its peer schools is Writing, and **the legitimacy of this year's oft-maligned Writing test** has been repeatedly questioned in the press. Accordingly, Lawrence's Academy's relatively poor performance on this single test, as compared to Lawrence's marked improvements in the other subject areas, should not be considered to reflect anything other than the previously acknowledged problems with the test itself.

The recently released Department of Education data reflects that Lawrence Academy has dramatically improved over the past year, exactly as Lawrence Academy predicted. Unfortunately, and for reasons completely independent of the quality of education Lawrence Academy provides, the "F" letter grade does not at all reflect that improvement. We believe that it would be unconscionable to deny Lawrence Academy's students, who made far greater strides over the past year than their peers at the other area schools, the opportunity to continue to advance their education at the school of their choice, solely because of a temporary, artificial drop in Lawrence Academy's letter grade. We are confident that, once you review the data, you will reach the same conclusion. We respectfully request, given the totality of the circumstances, that the School Board treat Lawrence Academy in a manner similar to the State Board of Education's direction during this year of transition and not draw conclusions solely on the letter grade this year.

Sincerely,

Albert E. Dotson, Jr.

AED/eo\3198925

cc:    Dr. Keitha Burnett
       Mrs. Althea King

# Appendix D
# (July 16, 2012 Letter to the District)

 Bilzin Sumberg
ATTORNEYS AT LAW

Albert E. Dotson, Jr., P.A.
Direct Dial: (305) 350-2411
Direct Fax: (305) 351-2217
Email: adotson@bilzin.com

July 16, 2012

Melinda L. McNichols, Esquire
Assistant School Board Attorney
Miami-Dade County School Board
1450 N.E. 2nd Avenue, Suite 430
Miami, Florida 33132.

      *Re:    Lawrence Academy*

Dear Ms. McNichols:

      I received your letter dated July 12, 2012 via e-mail and in the U.S. mail today responding to correspondence we previously sent to you on behalf of our client, Lawrence Academy.

      First, we are well aware of the "letter" (no pun intended) of the Settlement Agreement. However, as noted on the attached charts and in my letter, a copy of which is enclosed, use of the term "modest increase in [Lawrence Academy's] point total," significantly understates the progress that Lawrence Academy has made. Lawrence Academy's stellar educational record in connection with its middle school and high school has been unimpeached. Lawrence Academy's willingness to take on students who were part of a failed education program significantly expanded of our client's elementary school. Lawrence Academy chose not to cherry-pick its students. All of the statistics that the School Board has reflect that the longer a student is part of the Lawrence Academy system, the better that student performs. This fact continues to be ignored and hopefully, the mechanical application of the "letter" of the Settlement Agreement in a year where the efficacy and usefulness of the letter grades assigned to schools has been questioned by everyone -- to the point where the Commissioner of Education has placed a one-year moratorium on the full impact of the new grading system -- seems unjust, and ignores the facts "on the ground."

# APPENDICES

Lawrence Academy respectfully requests that the School Board reconsider. And, if the School Board decides not to acknowledge the progress and the admittedly unique circumstances, Lawrence Academy sincerely hopes that the students have access to a thriving academic environment committed, as Lawrence Academy demonstrated, to constant measurable improvement.

Sincerely,

Albert E. Dotson, Jr.

AED/eo
3207598.1

cc:    Alberto Carvalho, Superintendent
       Walter Harvey, Esquire, School Board Attorney
       Dr. Helen Blanch, Assistant Superintendent, Schools of Choice
       Tiffanie Pauline, Director of School Operations
       Dr. Keitha Burnett
       Althea King

# 2012 FCAT Math
# 3<sup>rd</sup> Grade

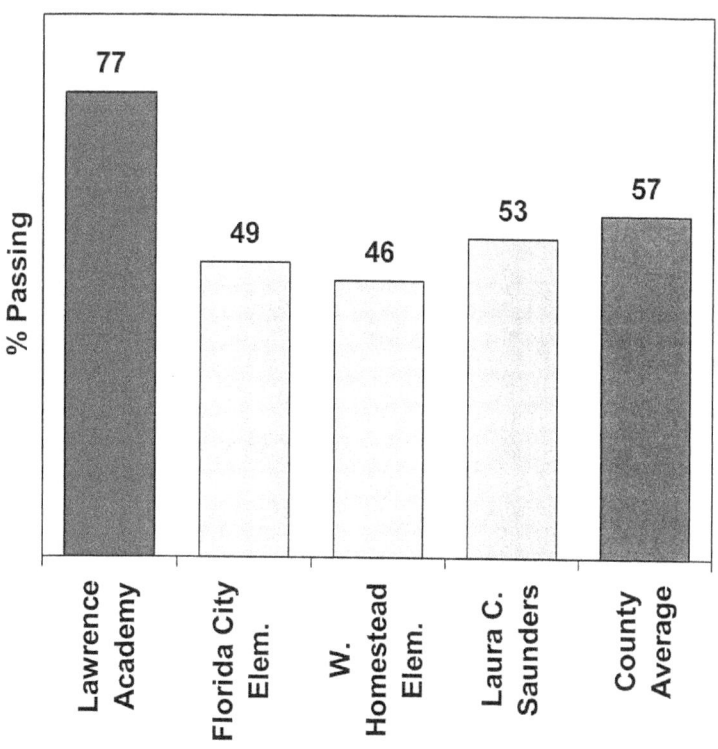

# 2012 FCAT Math
# Change from 2011
# 3rd Grade

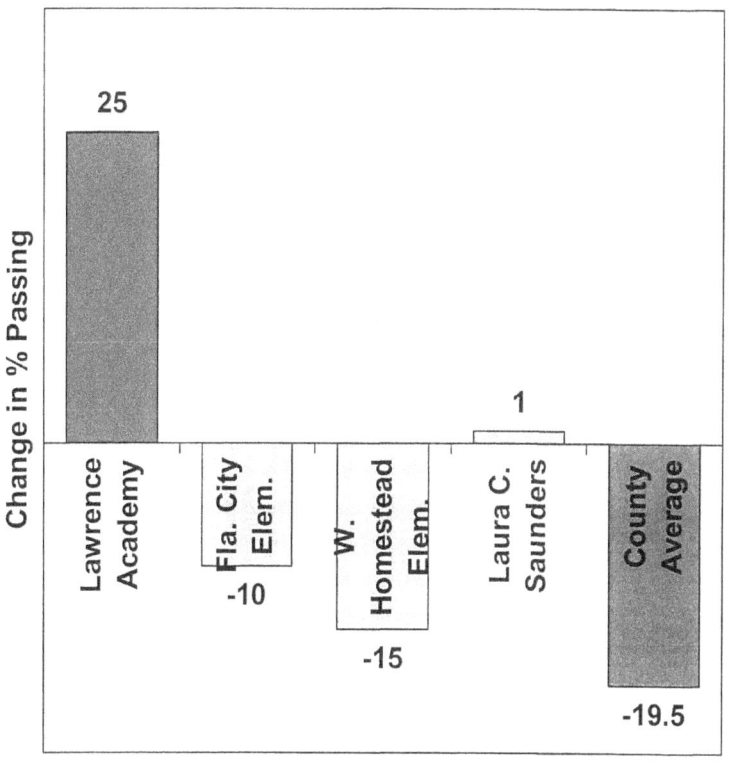

# 2012 FCAT Math
# Change from 2010
# 3rd Grade

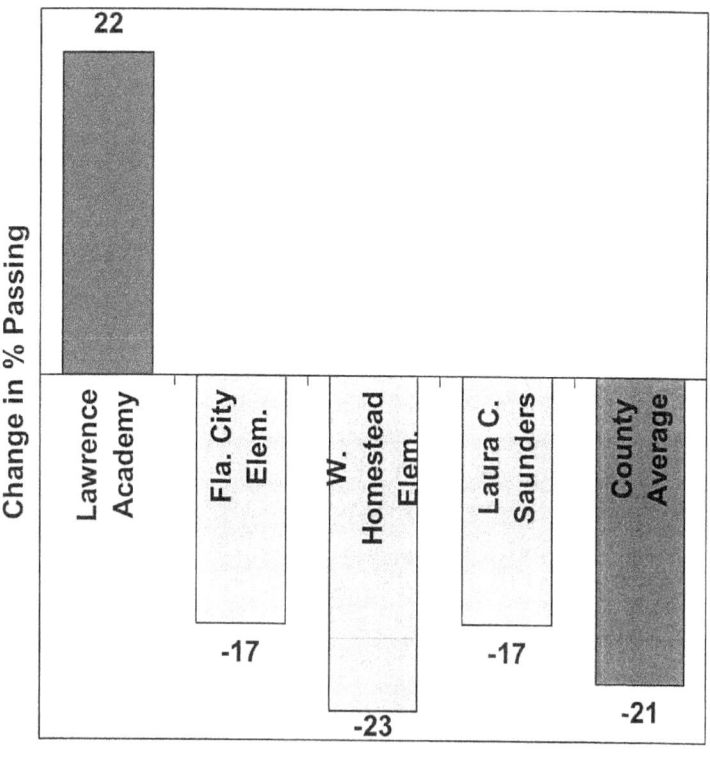

# 2012 FCAT Reading 3rd Grade

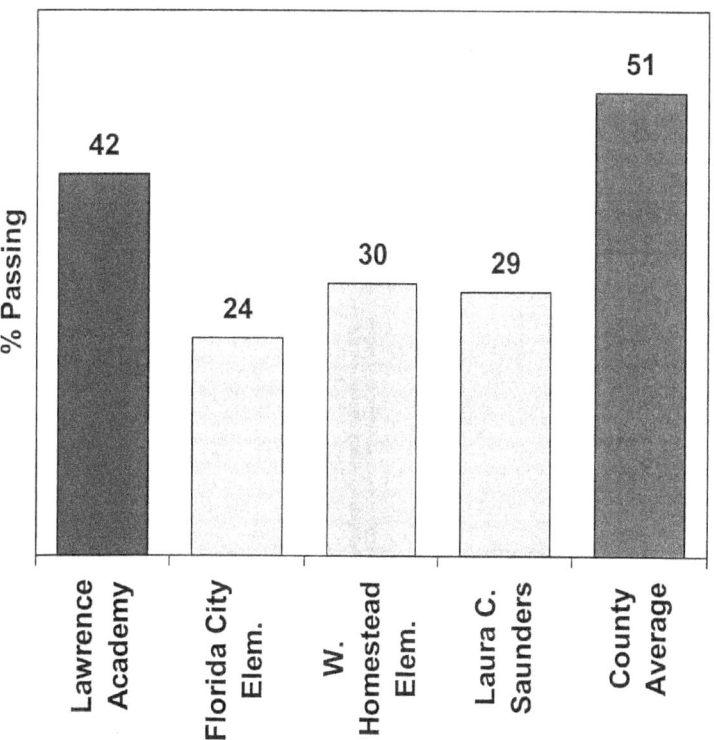

# 2012 FCAT Reading Change from 2011 3$^{rd}$ Grade

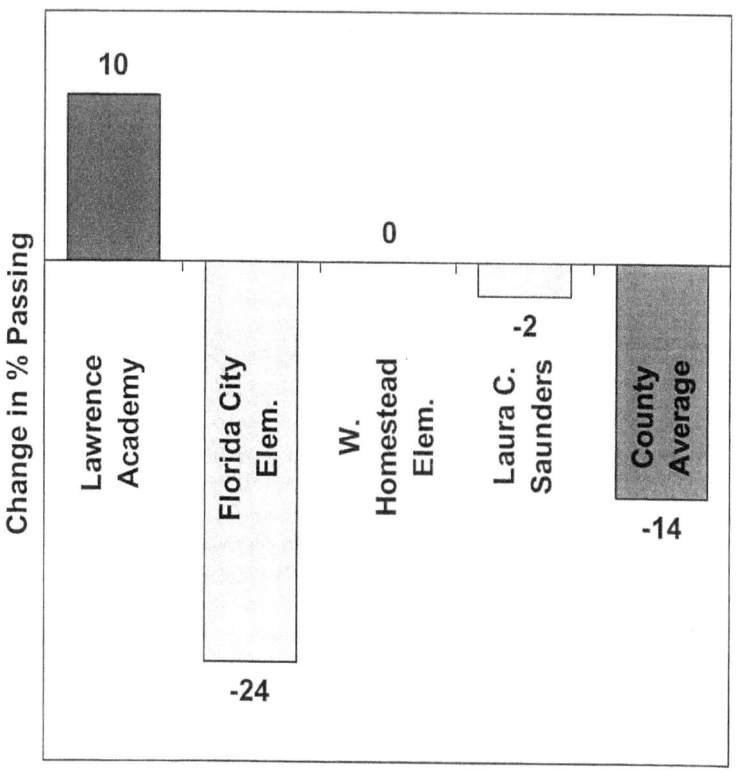

# 2012 FCAT Reading Change from 2010 3<sup>rd</sup> Grade

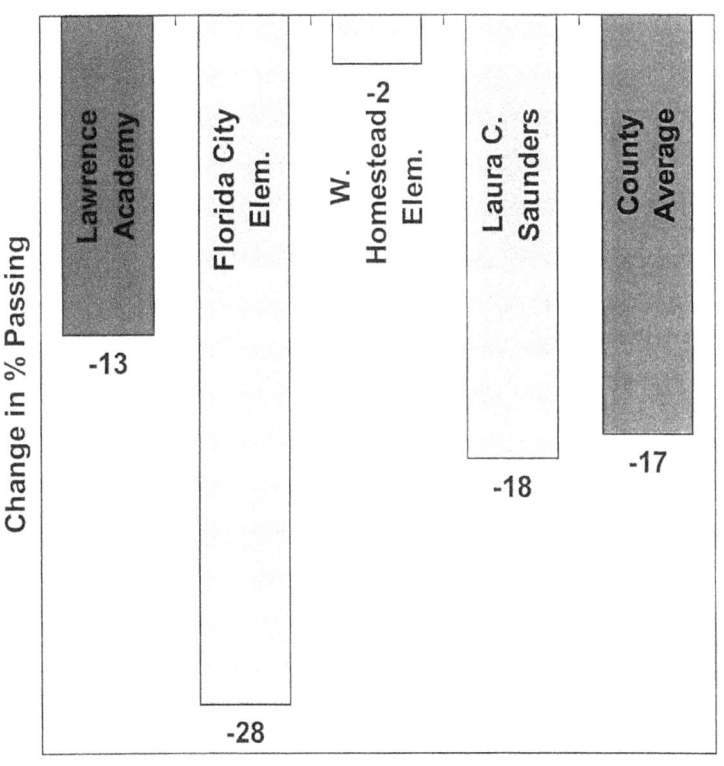

# 2012 FCAT Writing
## 4<sup>th</sup> Grade

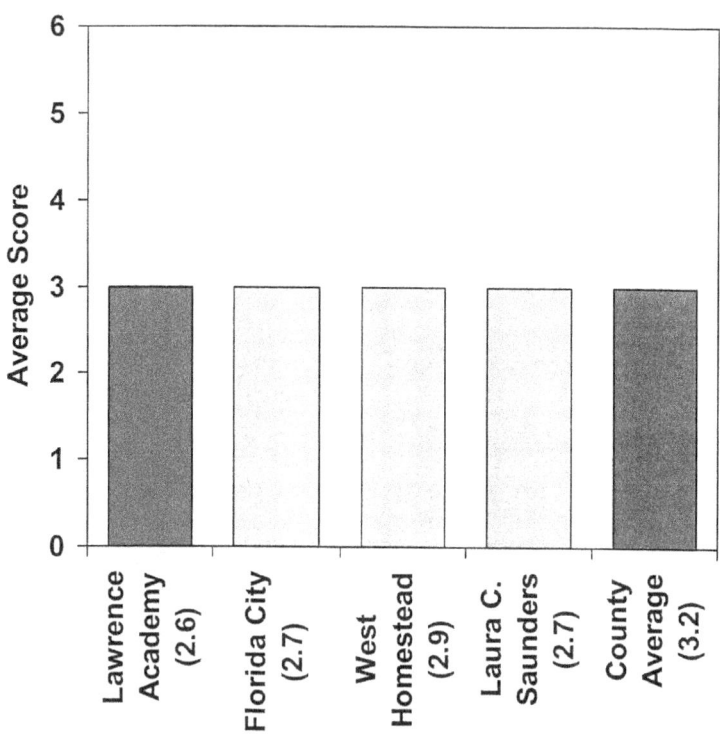

# 2012 FCAT Reading
# 4<sup>th</sup> Grade

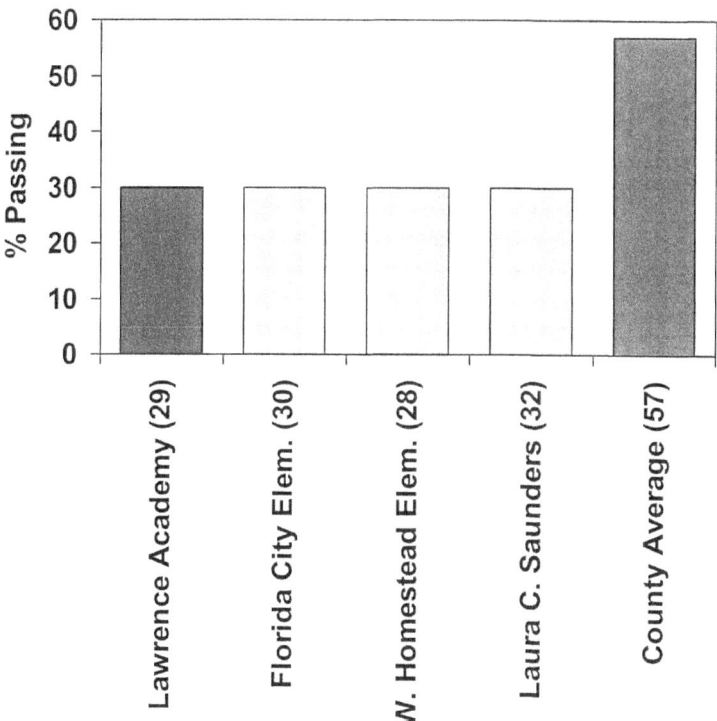

# 2012 FCAT Reading Change from 2011 4th Grade

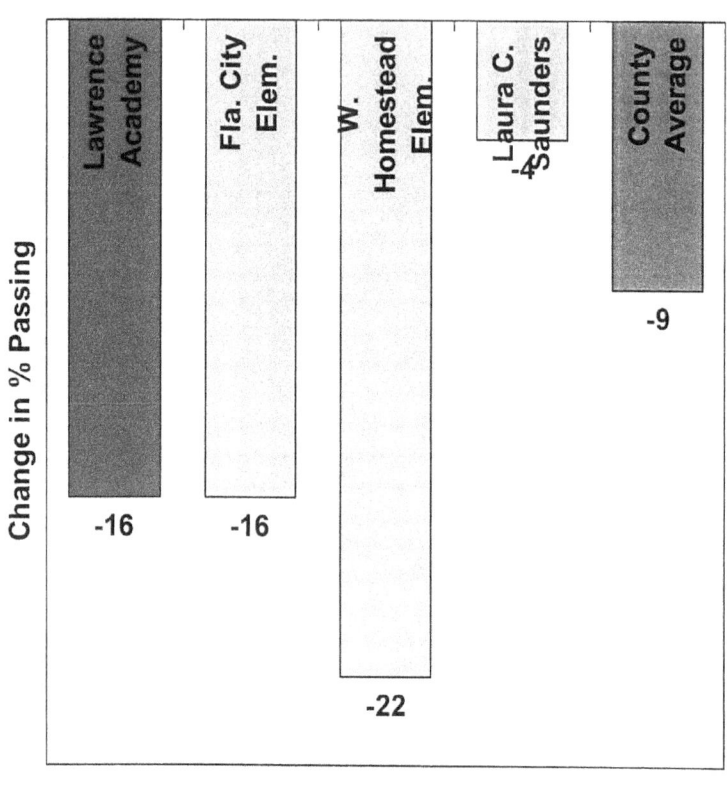

# 2012 FCAT Reading Change from 2010 4th Grade

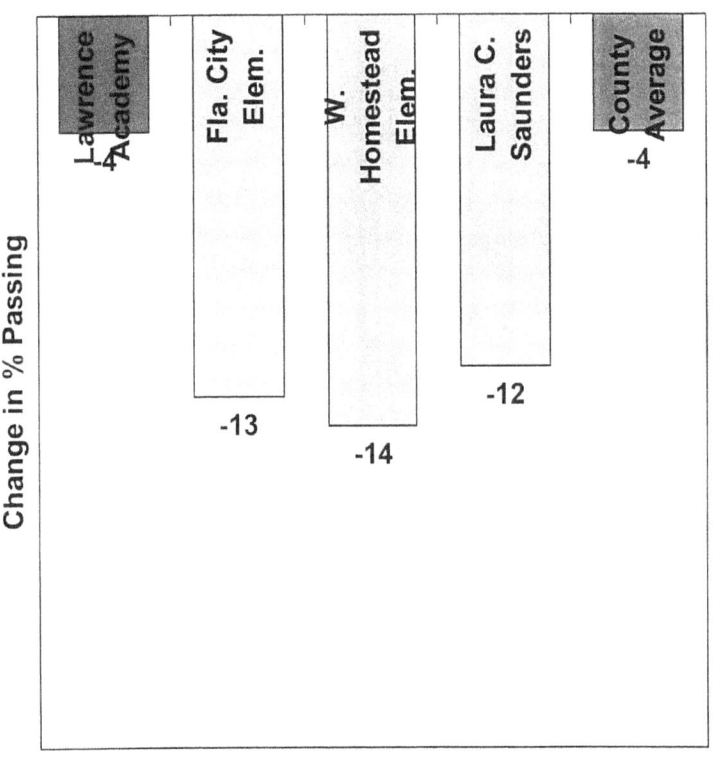

# 2012 FCAT Math
# 4th Grade

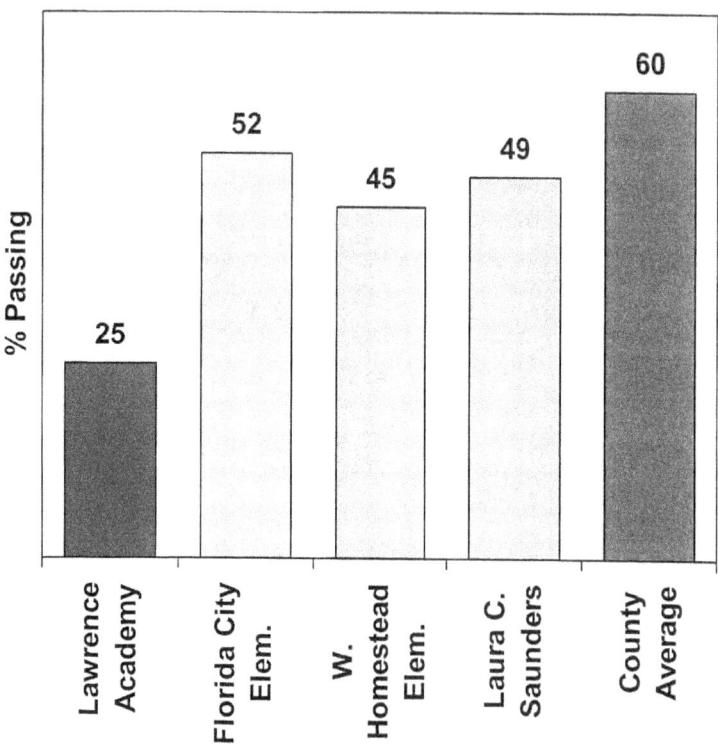

# 2012 FCAT Math Change from 2011 4<sup>th</sup> Grade

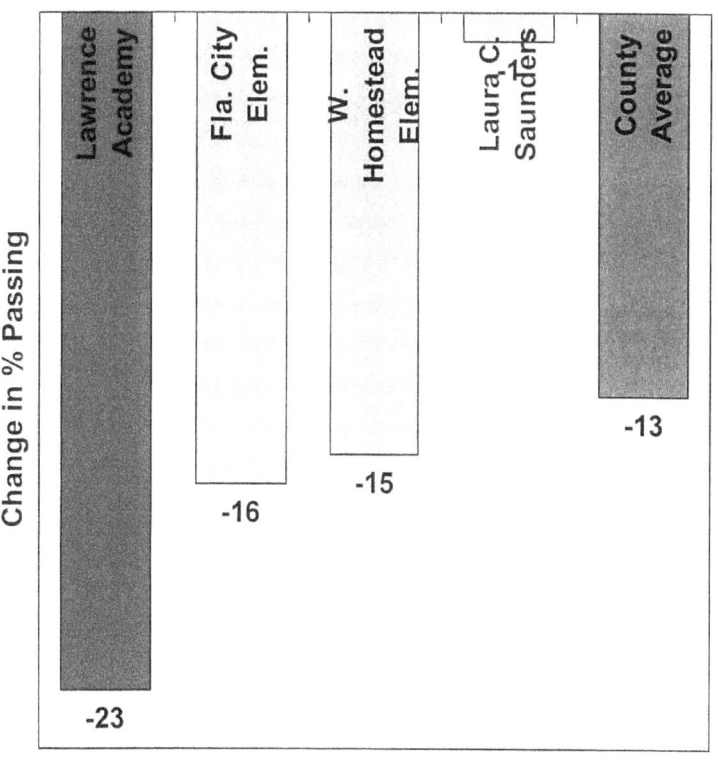

# 2012 FCAT Math
# Change from 2010
# 4<sup>th</sup> Grade

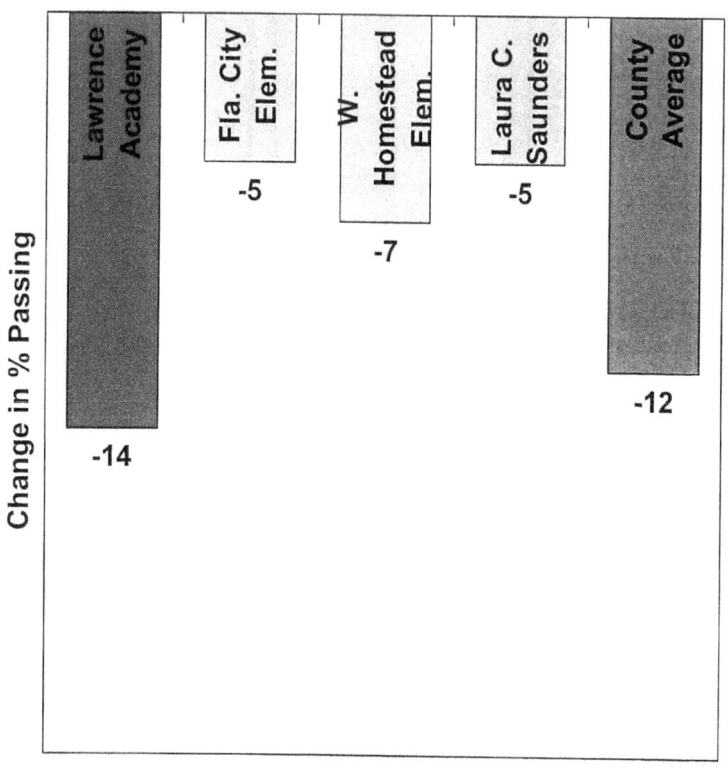

# 2012 FCAT Reading
# 5<sup>th</sup> Grade

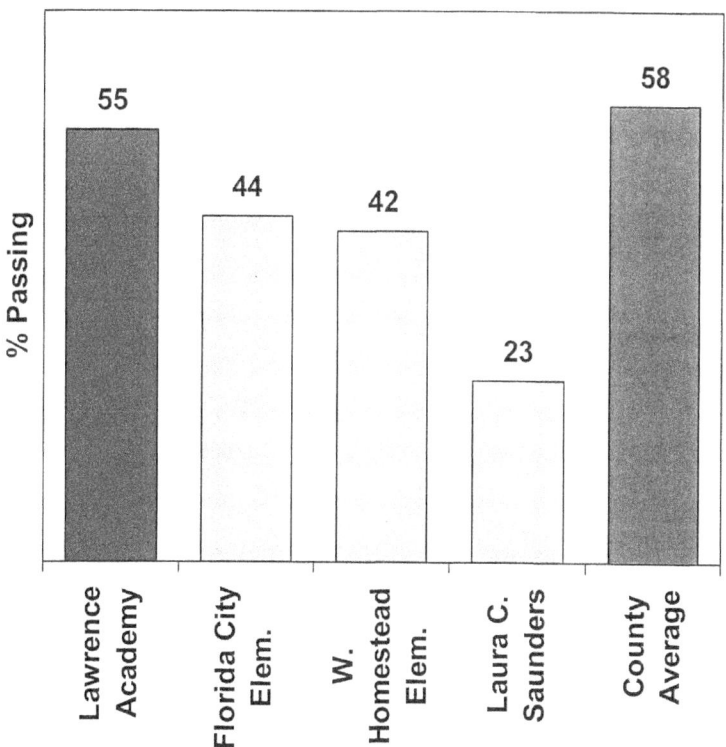

# 2012 FCAT Reading Change from 2011 5th Grade

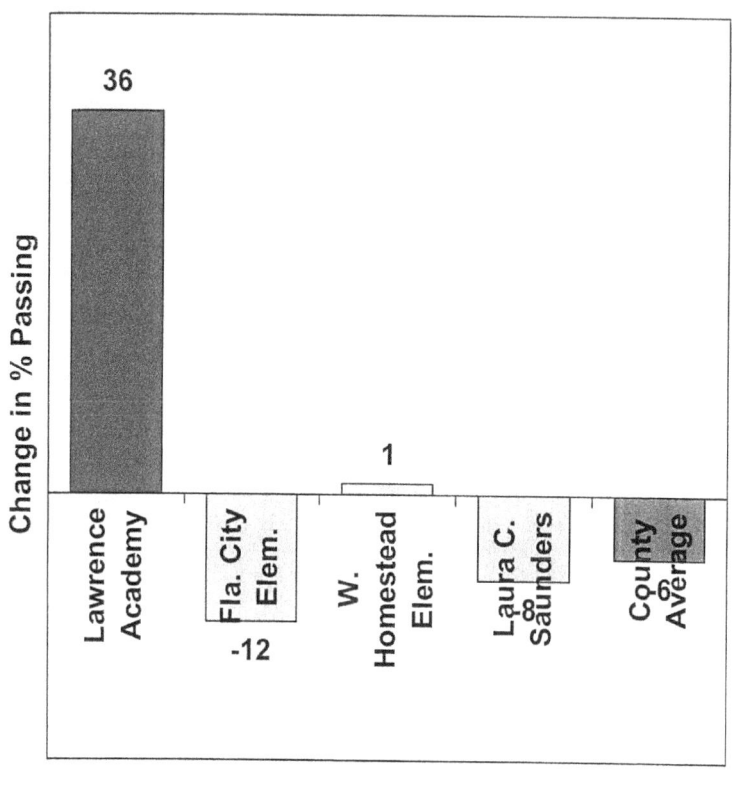

# 2012 FCAT Reading Change from 2010 5th Grade

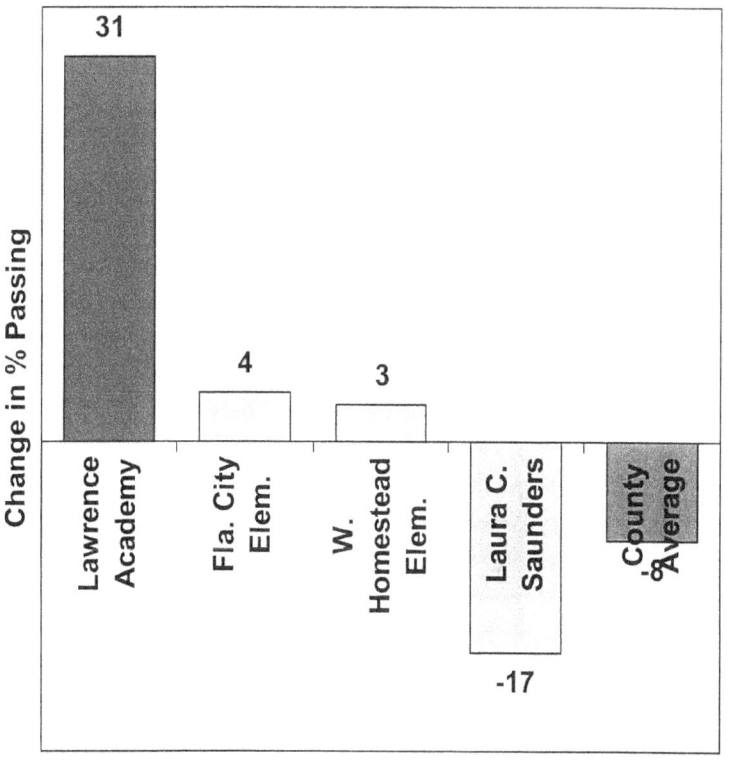

# 2012 FCAT Math
# 5th Grade

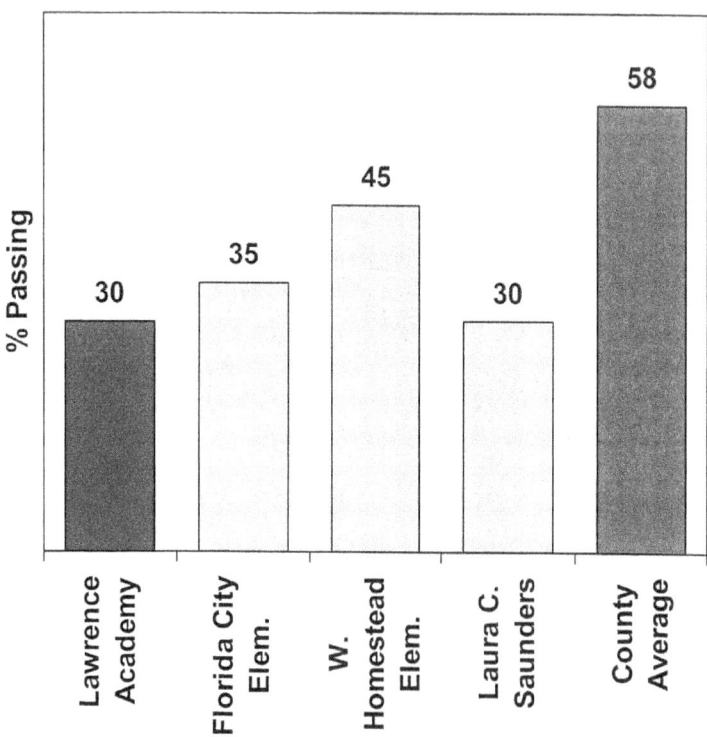

# 2012 FCAT Math
# Change from 2011
# 5th Grade

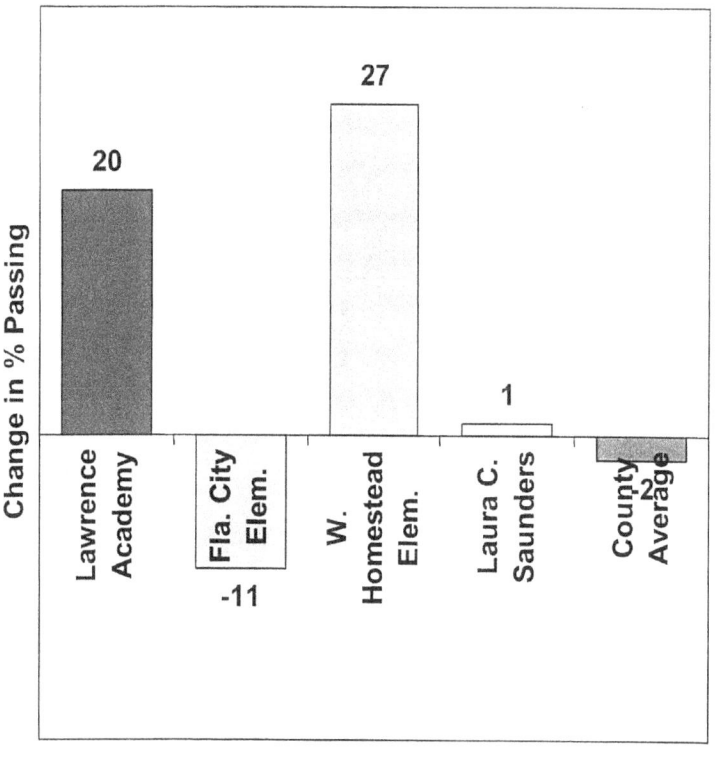

# 2012 FCAT Math
# Change from 2010
# 5th Grade

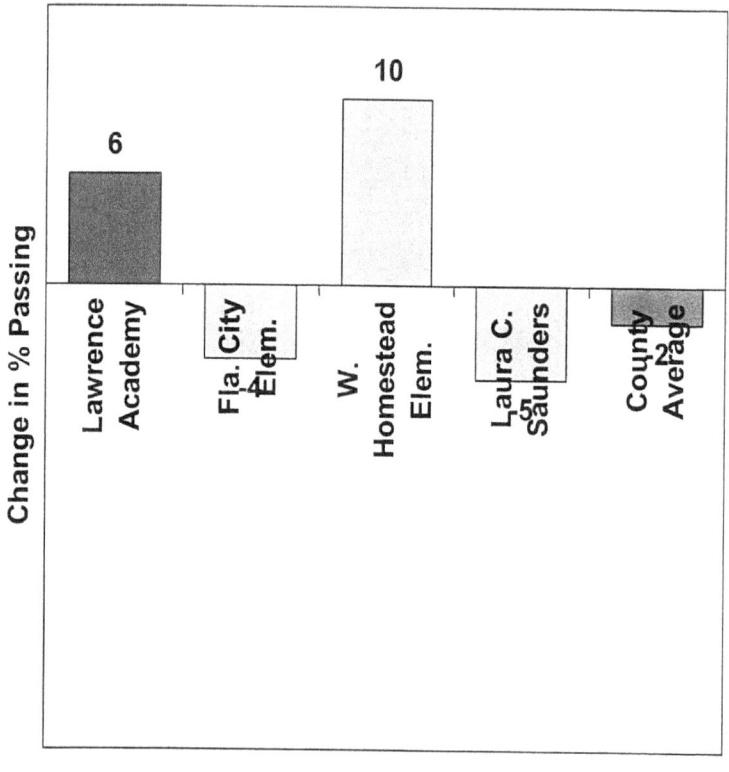

# 2012 FCAT Science 5th Grade

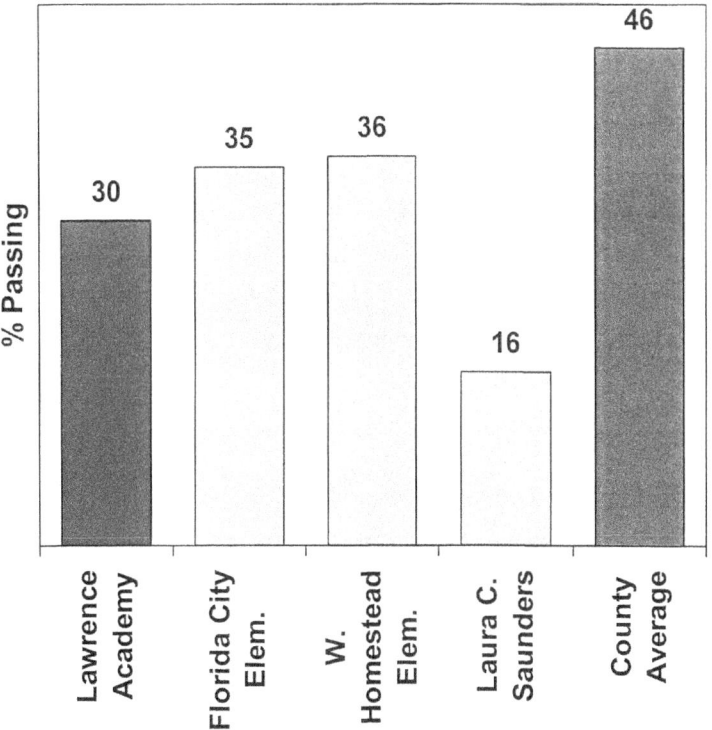

# 2012 FCAT Science
# Change from 2011
# 5th Grade

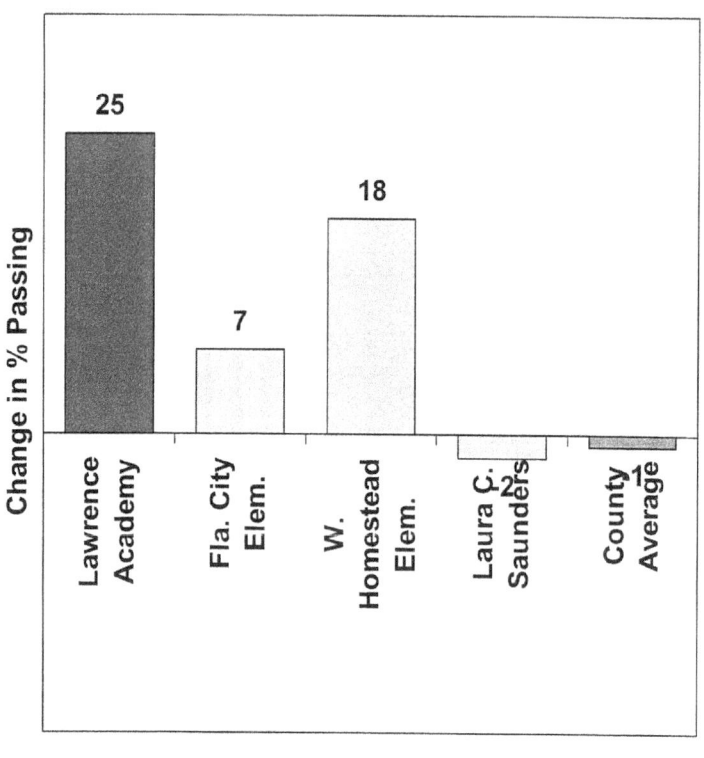

# 2012 FCAT Science
# Change from 2010
# 5th Grade

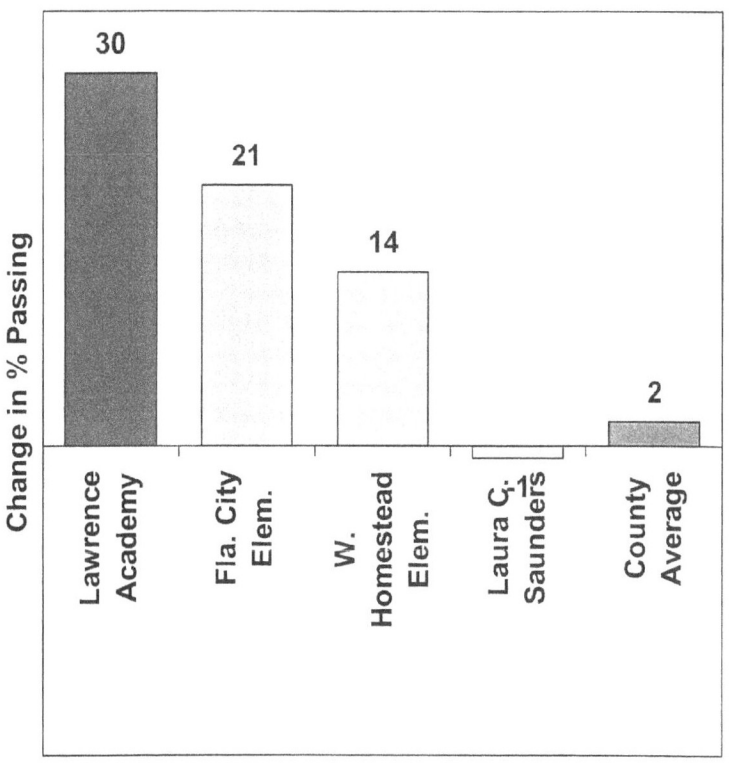

CPSIA information can be obtained
at www.ICGtesting.com
Printed in the USA
BVHW041049050419
544725BV00017B/432/P